CHIRICAHUA
MOUNTAINS

CHIRICAHUA MOUNTAINS

History and Nature

· WILLIAM ASCARZA ·

natural
HISTORY
PRESS

Published by Natural History Press
A Division of The History Press
Charleston, SC 29403
www.historypress.net

Front cover: Looking north toward Sugarloaf Mountain across the wonderland of standing-up rocks. *Courtesy of William Ascarza.*

First published 2014

Manufactured in the United States

ISBN 978.1.60949.800.9

Library of Congress CIP data applied for.

Notice: The information in this book is true and complete to the best of our knowledge. It is offered without guarantee on the part of the author or The History Press. The author and The History Press disclaim all liability in connection with the use of this book.

Contents

Acknowledgements

A special thank you goes out to Amerind Foundation; *Arizona Daily Star*; Arizona Geological Survey; Arizona Historical Society; Arizona-Sonora Desert Museum; Arizona State Museum; Armando M. Arvizu; Kevin Bays; Bisbee Mining & Historical Museum; Dan Caudle; my wife, Lorie Cavalli; Chiricahua Desert Museum; Chiricahua National Monument; Chiricahua Regional Museum & Research Center; Tom and Alicia Davidson; Douglas Historical Society; Flandrau Planetarium and Science Center; Fort Bowie National Historic Site; Freeport-McMoRan; Friends of the Pima County Public Library; Hardin-Simmons Photograph Collection; Henry F. Hauser Museum; Kyle E. Johnson; Library of Congress Prints and Photographs Division; Larry Ludwig; the late Orville Mickens and his Frontier Relics Museum; Suzanne Moody; National Archives and Records Administration; National Park Service Harpers Ferry Center Collections; Rex Allen Arizona Cowboy Museum; Santa Cruz Island Foundation; Sierra Vista Historical Society; Slaughter Ranch Johnson Historical Museum of the Southwest; United States Department of Agriculture; University of Arizona Library; U.S. Navy National Museum of Naval Aviation; Rafael Velasco; and Western Archaeological Conservation Center.

Introduction

The Chiricahua Mountains are an undiscovered country in southeastern Arizona. Pronounced cheery-cow-ah, the name Chiricahua may have been derived from an Opata Indian word, *Chiguicagui*, which means "mountain of the wild turkeys." To the Apache, the Chiricahua Mountains were defined as Big Mountain. The term "Cherry Cows" was a corruption of Chiricahua. The term dated back to the early 1880s, having been used at times to refer to the mountain range, the Apache, the twenty thousand head of cattle that roamed nearby the range in the 1920s and also a mining camp.

The Chiricahua Mountains are a remote mountain range in Arizona located 125 miles southeast of Tucson. Composed of unique rock formations, elevation gains of over nine thousand feet above sea level and dense vegetation, the Chiricahua Mountains are a significant sky island harboring diverse wildlife and unique plant species. Inhabited at various times by Apache, homesteaders, U.S. military encampments, miners, outlaws and current residents, this range has retained its allure through the years. Having sustained extreme heat, drought and fire over the course of history, the Chiricahua Mountain range remains a popular destination for birders, campers, hikers and researchers.

As part of the Coronado National Forest in southeastern Arizona, the Chiricahua Mountains are located in the Douglas district. The Coronado National Forest includes four other districts, including Nogales, Safford, Santa Catalina and Sierra Vista. Altogether, the five districts encompass nearly two million acres of land spread out among the many mountain ranges in southeastern Arizona. The Chiricahua Mountains are one of the many sky islands that make up the land mass of southeastern Arizona. A sky island is defined as an isolated mountain range rising above the surrounding grasslands, similar to an island surrounded by the sea. When one flies over southeastern Arizona or looks at topographic maps and satellite imagery of the region, he or she will notice a series of north–south tending mountain ranges divided by valley. This topography is known as the Basin and Range Province, which was created by crustal thinning and stretching, and it is uniquely found in the western United States.

The Chiricahua Mountains are part of the Madrean Archipelago stretching from central Mexico into southern Arizona. Named because of its resemblance to an oceanic archipelago or sea dotted by islands, the region includes a collection of forty neighboring mountain ranges that lay between the Colorado Plateau and the Sierra Madre Occidental—essentially a grassland dotted by mountains. In the Chiricahua Mountains, the Sonoran and Chihuahuan deserts and the Rocky Mountain and Sierra Madre ranges all meet. Many flora and fauna found in the Chiricahua Mountains are also found in the Sierra Madrean range in Mexico, the Rocky Mountains to the north and other neighboring mountain ranges in Arizona and New Mexico. The Chiricahua Mountains have an interesting geologic history with both diverse plant and animal life combined with a documented historical record that includes habitation from the early Hohokam, Apache, Spanish and finally American settlers.

Logistically, the Chiricahua Mountains are a remote sky island. Located forty-nine miles northwest of the Chiricahua Mountains, the town of Willcox is the nearest sizable population. Contained by surrounding highways and valleys, the Chiricahua Mountain Range is accessible from all directions. U.S. Highway 80, located on the east side of the Chiricahua Mountain Range, allows for easy access to Cave Creek and the town of Portal. It connects the town of Road Forks, New Mexico, off Interstate 10, with Douglas, Arizona. San Bernardino Valley is located southeast of the Chiricahua Mountains. U.S. Highway 191 northbound and Interstate Highway 10 cross through San Simon Valley, which boundaries the north and eastern part of the Chiricahua Mountain Range. Access to the Chiricahua Mountains may also be obtained by driving the Portal–San Simon Portal Road accessible from Interstate 10. The seventeen-mile dirt road leads directly to Portal with an accessible turnoff to the west to the town of Paradise after the twentieth mile. To reach Chiricahua National Monument from Tucson, take Interstate 10 East to Willcox, then take Arizona highway 186 south from Willcox to junction 181. Turn left on 181 East. After four miles, the exit to Pinery Canyon Road to the right becomes an option within several hundred feet from the National Monument entrance.

The geography and topography of the Chiricahua Mountains are as vast as they are diverse. The Chiricahua Mountains are a bow-shaped range of inactive volcanoes twenty miles wide and forty miles long. The southern part of the Chiricahua Mountains is often referred to as the Pedregosa Mountains, while the northern extent of the range reaches just south of Fort Bowie. The base of the Chiricahua Mountains in the Chihuahuan Desert is 3,600 feet with prevalent grassland, while its highpoint is Chiricahua Peak, reaching 9,796 feet and covered with Douglas fir and ponderosa pine. Chiricahua Peak is the second-highest mountain peak in southeastern Arizona next to Mount Graham, which rises 10,720 feet above sea level in the Pinaleño Mountain Range. The Chiricahua Mountains are the largest "sky island" mountain range in the Coronado National Forest. Chiricahua Peak and nearby Fly Peak are accessible by the five-mile Crest Trail, the trailhead of which is accessible from Rustler Park from the Pinery Canyon Road just before entering Chiricahua National Monument. Rustler Park, the largest meadow in the Chiricahua Mountains, covers five acres of land and a campground that is managed by the forest service.

The scarcity of water deposits in southeastern Arizona makes the natural supply of underground water in the Chiricahua Mountains an important source for people, flora and fauna alike. Shake Spring, located in the middle of Bonita Canyon, provides the Chiricahua National Monument with the most reliable source of water. Additional reliable springs with year-round water availability in the Chiricahua Mountains include Anita, Booger, Bear, Eagle, Mormon and Ojo Aqua Fria Springs. Fractured and porous limestone outcrops found in the Chiricahua Mountains allow water seepage from rain to permeate the soil and recharge the aquifers. Water runs in Bonita Creek off and on throughout the year, depending on the amount of rainfall. Water runs in the creek after a summer monsoon for anywhere from several hours up to several days. During the winter and early spring, depending on snowmelt and water runoff, the creek can run several weeks at a time.

Weather patterns in the Chiricahua Mountains vary depending on elevation. A standard rule for mountain sky islands states that the higher the elevation, the greater the precipitation and snow accumulation, which contrasts to warmer and drier climate found in lower elevations of the Chiricahua Mountain Range. Temperature in the high elevations is similar to the cool temperatures found in the forests of Canada. As a general rule, every four feet of elevation gain equates to walking one mile northward. Vegetation differs depending on location on a slope. Desert vegetation tends to favor south-facing slopes because of increased sun exposure, and high evaporation north-facing slopes favor greener vegetation with a greater tree count.

Rainfall patterns in the American Southwest are related to sea surface temperatures in the Pacific Ocean. El Niño occurs when sea surface temperatures in the eastern Pacific Ocean near the equator are warmer than usual. This causes winters to be wetter than normal. La Niña occurs when sea surface temperatures in the eastern Pacific Ocean near the equator are cooler than usual. This causes winters to be drier than normal. Winter storms originate in the North Pacific Ocean. Rainfall patterns in the Chiricahua Mountains vary greatly depending on elevation and season. Annual precipitation ranges from as little as 8.0 inches in the valley bottom to as much as 40.0 inches on the summit. The average annual precipitation in the Chiricahua Mountains is 19.3 inches. Every one-thousand-foot increase in elevation results in a 3.0- to 4.0-inch increase in annual precipitation. Rustler Park can average 27.0 inches of rain per year in contrast to Rucker Canyon, which averages 12.0 inches of rain per year.

The summer monsoon is categorized by violent thunderstorms, while the winter season receives gentle rains. Monsoonal storms derive their moisture from two sources: the Pacific Ocean and the Gulf of California. Temperatures can reach in excess of one hundred degrees Fahrenheit. The dry period in the spring is more stressful than the fall dry period because of the increasing temperatures in the spring. One-half of the annual precipitation occurs between July and September, while the other half occurs in November through March. Tropical storms sometimes affect the Southwest in the fall, bringing daylong periods of steady precipitation.

Different biotic communities encompass the Chiricahua Mountains, including those found in the Sonoran and Chihuahuan deserts, the Sierra Madre and the Rocky Mountains. Alpine views abound across the higher elevations of the Chiricahua Mountain Range. Grasses dominate their foothills. Springs are found where groundwater flows to the surface. Over nine springs have been found within Chiricahua National Monument. Hand-dug wells have been discovered around Faraway Ranch, where inhabitants sought out a year-round supply of underground water. The two major drainages that occur on the western slopes of Chiricahua National Monument are Bonita Creek and Rhyolite Creek. As part of Coronado National Forest, the Chiricahua Mountains are protected from mining and logging interests.

The general history of the Chiricahua Mountains pertains to its documented human habitation and the countries that have overseen its jurisdiction. Earliest documented evidence of habitation in the Chiricahua Mountains consists of a Clovis archaeological area in the Whitewater Draw tributary known as the Double Adobe Site. This and other sites, including Cave Creek Canyon, date back three thousand years. The dependable water at this site and other sites in the Chirichau Mountains sustained Native American populations through modern history. While the Chiricahua Mountains have been cited among archaeological circles as having been inhabited by Native Americans several thousand years ago, the recorded history begins with the arrival of the Coronado expedition, which journeyed through this land in search of the renowned seven cities of Cibola in 1540.

The interaction between the Spanish and the nomadic group of Native Americans known as the Apache who had arrived in the area just prior to the Spanish in the 1600s ushered in an era of instability in the regions that would continue until the surrender of Geronimo in 1886. The Apache were known as hunters, gatherers and raiders. In 1682, Apache made their first reported raid into the land of what is known today as Mexico. From this moment on up until the early 1930s, both Apache and Spanish (later the Mexicans) held disdain for one another.

By 1768, the Apache had launched a major offensive against the Spanish in Sonora, resulting in an increase in warfare between the two forces that was not pacified until the peace of 1786. The Spanish erected a presidio in San Bernardino Valley in 1774. The territory that became Arizona was acquired from Mexico in 1848 and 1853. The Treaty of Guadalupe Hidalgo on February 2, 1848, ended the Mexican War. As a result, Mexico ceded Texas, California, Utah, Colorado, Wyoming, New Mexico and Arizona north of the Gila River. The United States' intent to establish a transcontinental railroad to connect the eastern states along the southern route with the gold fields of California necessitated the Gadsden Purchase, signed on December 30, 1853, and ratified by Congress on June 30, 1854. This enabled the United States to establish a permanent presence in southeastern Arizona. The United States paid $10 million to Mexico for these valuable 29,670 square miles. Gray Mountain in the Chiricahua Mountains was named for Andrew Belcher Gray, the principal surveyor with John Russell Bartlett's Boundary Commission, who was instrumental in plotting the future route of the Southern Pacific Railroad. While involved in plotting the boundary survey in what later became southeastern Arizona, Gray camped at the Cave Creek Cienega in the Chiricahua Mountains in 1854. The following decade, the Chiricahua Mountains proved a formidable bastion for the Apache, who were by then conducting a full-fledged war against Anglo settlement precipitated by the Bascom Affair. Conflicts between settlers and Apache continued into the late nineteenth century and did not subside until Geronimo surrendered in September 1886 and the majority of Apache were removed first to Florida and then to reservations in Oklahoma and New Mexico. However, occasional skirmishes and sightings of remnant Apache continued in southeastern Arizona into the 1890s. Fort Rucker and Fort Bowie served as bases from which the U.S. military could strike back against the raiding parties of Apache. Ranching and mining communities became prevalent after the removal of the Apache, and homesteading also grew in popularity. Despite some success in mineral exploration, the Chiricahua Mountains never became a major producer of minerals like some of the neighboring localities, including Bisbee and Morenci. However, some metals were discovered and successfully mined, in places such as the Hilltop Mine.

Bandits and bootleggers made their mark in the Chiricahua Mountains. During the 1870s through the 1920s, the mountains were the scene of stashed

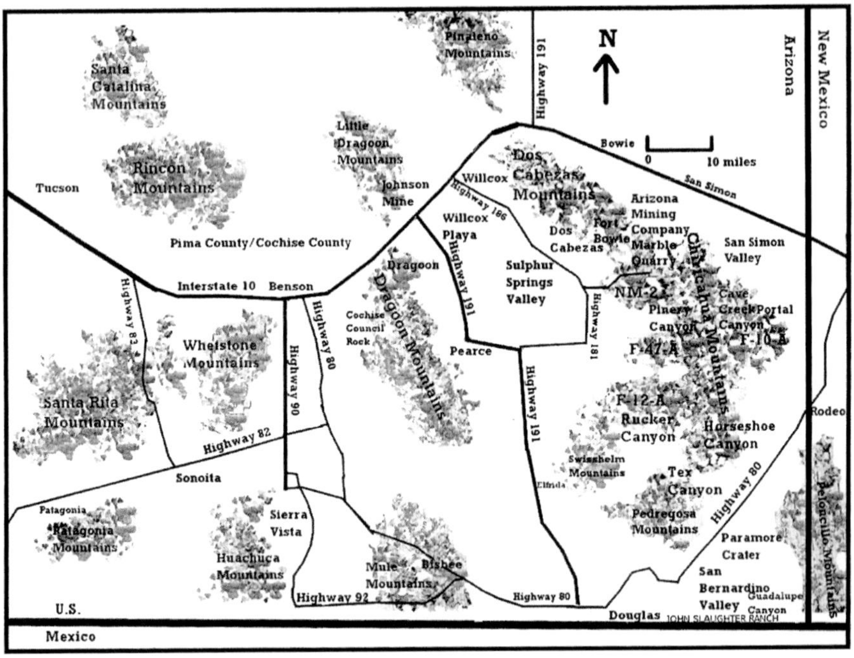

Map I shows the Chiricahua Mountains in relation to southeastern Arizona. The Civilian Conservation Corps camps that operated in the Chiricahua Mountains are prominently displayed. *Courtesy of William Ascarza.*

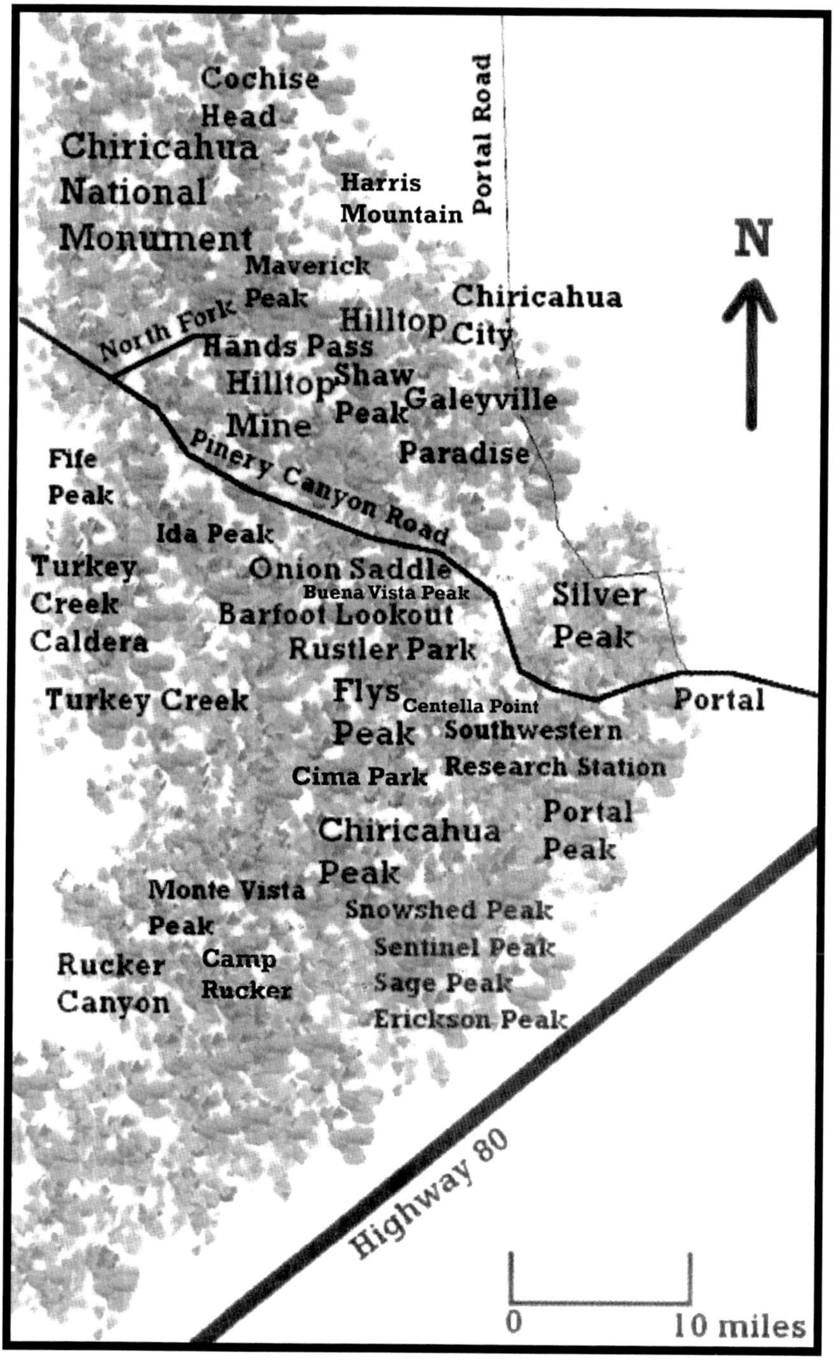

Map II, seen here, depicts important localities in the Chiricahua Mountains. *Courtesy of William Ascarza.*

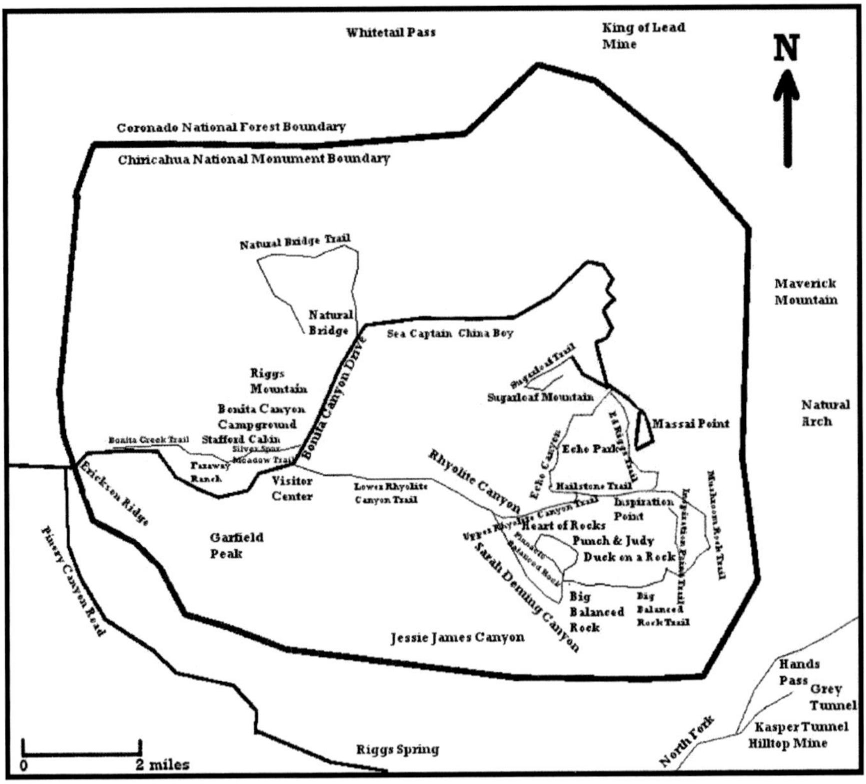

Map III highlights trails found in Chiricahua National Monument. It also provides a visual boundary between the Chiricahua National Monument and the Coronado National Forest Boundary. Several prominent mines are also seen outside of the Chiricahua National Monument. *Courtesy of William Ascarza.*

loot from armed robberies. By 1915, Arizona had imposed a prohibition on the sale of alcoholic beverages statewide. However, New Mexico remained a state where alcoholic beverages were readily available. The Chiricahua Mountains became a passageway for bootleggers transporting alcohol from Rodeo, New Mexico, to San Simon Valley, Arizona. What became known as "Bootlegger Saddle" was a ridge between Pinery Canyon and Rock Creek. Mule trains were the mode of transportation for whiskey passing through Barfoot Park into West Turkey Creek. A fire lookout was built in nearby Buena Vista Peak, which attains an elevation of 8,823 feet.

The Civilian Conservation Corps played an integral role in the development of the Chiricahua Mountains. With the onset of the Great Depression in the 1930s and the scarcity of work in many areas across

This aerial image of the Chiricahua Mountains was taken at a flight altitude of thirty thousand feet. *Courtesy of William Ascarza.*

the country, needful work projects sponsored by the U.S. government were implemented to improve the land. Much of the work of the CCC in the Chiricahua Mountains involved both water-related activities and fire protection. It is the CCC that was responsible for digging wells, erosion control, development of water areas for stock and stream development. The corps was also responsible for building several fire control lookout towers in the Chiricahua Mountains.

Today, the Chiricahua Mountains are recovering from the Horseshoe 2 Fire, which affected a large percentage of the range. Despite the intensity of the fire, the Chiricahua Mountains still retain their beauty and presence. Although the fire has removed large portions of timber in the range, the views are spectacular and have even been somewhat improved with the removal of the high-density woodland that had previously provided cover.

Chapter 1

Geology

The geologic record of the Chiricahua Mountains part of the Basin and Range Province involves plate tectonics, the movement of the earth's plates, which caused subduction, compression and extension of the earth's crust. This led to a high frequency of earthquakes and volcanic activity in western North America. The earth is composed of plates that slide past or subduct with one another on contact. The lighter, westward-moving North American plate, composed of granite, impacted the denser basaltic oceanic plate. The result was subduction, in which the denser oceanic rock subducted beneath the lighter granite rock. As the oceanic rock sunk, both rock and water increased in temperature and began to melt upon mixing with hot mantle rock. The molten rock had to travel out, similar to steam in a kettle, and, in this case, upward in the form of magma chambers several miles below the surface of the earth. As the magma reached the earth's surface, it caused the collapse of these magma chambers, ultimately forming calderas.

One of these magma chambers was located just south of the present Chiricahua National Monument twenty-seven million years ago. It ruptured, expelling molten rock, carbon dioxide and water vapor. The reduction of magma from beneath the surface caused the collapse of the magma chamber. The impact of the steam and gas explosions instigated massive clouds known as nuée ardente, along with lahaars composed of burning gas, pumice and lava flowing down the slopes of the caldera with the force of an avalanche at speeds in excess of one hundred miles per hour. The material that was ejected from the volcano formed much of the bedrock found around Chiricahua National Monument. This material is classified as tuff or Rhyolite Canyon Tuff (silica-rich rhyolite) measuring in excess of eight hundred feet thick. The superheated siliceous ash and pumice melted together and hardened, forming rhyolite. Magma with a high percentage of silica is known as rhyolite. The eruption spewed over 100 cubic miles of magma covering an area of 1,200 square miles. The ash circled the entire world, impacting the weather with a decline in global temperature.

This massive circular depression, known by locals as the Turkey Creek Caldera, remains to this day. Located in the middle of the Chiricahua Mountains, the Turkey Creek Caldera was formed by a volcanic eruption that was one thousand times greater than the May 1980 Mount St. Helens eruption in Washington State. The volcanic eruption that formed the Turkey Creek Caldera also measured between five and ten times the size of the Krakatoa volcano of 1883. After the initial explosion, the Turkey Creek Caldera has been estimated to be twice as large as the Crater Lake Caldera located in Crater Lake National Park, Oregon. Its measurements are estimated at twelve miles in diameter and five thousand feet deep above the magma chamber. Over time, subsequent faulting and erosion, along with pumice and ash from the initial eruption, has obscured the Turkey Creek Caldera, located eight miles south of the Chiricahua National Monument. Chiricahua, Buena Vista, Ida, Sentinel and Fly's Peaks are remnants of the Turkey Creek Caldera that was named after a nearby stream. The rocks produced by the volcano rhyolite ash-flow tuff reveal its past existence. The Chiricahua Mountains were formed by multiple volcanic eruptions that produced abundant volcanic ash in excess of two hundred cubic miles.

Subduction off the western coast of North America slowed as the East Pacific ocean ridge collided with the subduction zone. Subduction subsided, causing a decrease of volcanism in the American Southwest. The forces of extension (from crustal thinning) produced high-angle faulting, causing blocks or graben to drop, forming valleys between the mountain ranges commonly seen today when flying over southeastern Arizona in an airplane. Slow uplift fractured the volcanic rock in the area over the past twenty million years, creating many of the unique rock formations found in Chiricahua National Monument.

In Chiricahua National Monument, the geology is apparent in every aspect, especially with regard to rhyolite. The hills north and south of Faraway Ranch are composed of rhyolite formed from a lava flow. A remnant of the Turkey Creek Caldera can be seen from the high ground in Chiricahua National Monument atop Sugarloaf Mountain. The rhyolite outcrops can be found along the boundary of the caldera. Rhyolite Canyon and Sugarloaf Mountain are the product of individual volcanic eruptions. Located northeast of Chiricahua National Monument and evident from atop Sugarloaf Mountain, Cochise Head is a mile-long monolith monument of sculpted rhyolite. Rhyolite Canyon Tuff is a thick volcanic ash deposit caused by the eruption that created the Turkey Creek Caldera. This material covers most of the National Monument.

When hiking around Massai Point and Echo Canyon in Chiricahua National Monument, several thousand rock columns and joints are visible. These vertical joints that formed in welded tuff are susceptible to the entry of water, instigating chemical and physical weathering. These processes caused the formation of hoodoos and spires. Different rates of weathering exist in these rock structures due to ice, water and wind. Rain and snowmelt from higher elevations flow down the steep canyons, causing fractures in the rock and alluvium of canyon bottoms. Joints and cracks in rhyolite were caused by cooling and uplifting.

Wind and water caused the erosion that formed the balanced rocks. Rocks such as Big Balanced Rock were sculpted over time by the forces of erosion. Another example of unique erosion in Chiricahua National Monument is the Natural Bridge, a bridge of welded rhyolite tuff viewed from the overlook located at the end of the Natural Bridge Trail. The Natural Bridge was formed during the Pleistocene glacial period by flowing water and wind that eroded the rock beneath the bridge. Another similarly named formation found in the eastern Chiricahua Mountains located on private property in East Whitetail Canyon near the town of Paradise is the fifteen-foot Natural Arch or Whitetail Arch, which is, in fact, an opening eroded through a mass of basalt rock.

Characteristic trademarks of the Chiricahua Mountains are their pinnacles and cliffs, a sought-after and accessible sight for visitors in Chiricahua National Monument. Formed by case hardening caused by the amorphous silica left behind after precipitated water evaporates off the surface of the rock formations, pinnacles in Chiricahua National Monument were formed by the freezing and thawing of water during the last ice age approximately ten thousand years ago. Cooler and wetter conditions were more the norm back then, in contrast to the warmer and drier climate of the present. Hoodoos are columns that have a prescribed thickness and often appear totem pole–shaped. The rock formations in Chiricahua National Monument are stable. Pinnacles can endure thirteen times their weight in stress prior to collapsing. According to data gleaned from seismometers, although unaffected by road maintenance, rock climbing has been found

One of the many balanced rocks composed of rhyolite awaits visitors as they hike the trails in Chiricahua National Monument. *Courtesy of National Park Service Harpers Ferry Center Collections.*

to cause rock fall and has therefore been banned in the confines of the Chiricahua National Monument.

Many different types of rocks exist in the Chiricahua Mountains, some of the most common of which are rhyolite, andesite, dacite and basalt. Large talus slides of rocks are commonly found throughout many of the canyons in

Peering through the pinnacles (or hoodoos) in Chiricahua National Monument along the Echo Canyon Trail provides a spectacular view. *Courtesy of William Ascarza.*

A narrow view of a distant balanced rock is afforded to hikers along the Echo Canyon Trail. *Courtesy of William Ascarza.*

the Chiricahua Mountains. The oldest rocks in the Chiricahua Mountains are Pinal Schist, a metamorphic rock that formed 1.7 billion years ago during the Precambrian era. The oldest rocks in Chiricahua National Monument are found as exposed fault block in the northeast corner of the monument. These are Paleozoic Permian limestone formed 280 million years ago. A good place to view rhyolite tuff is the drive along Bonita Canyon Highway. Dark andesite and basalt also appear along the highway as it journeys to Massai Point and Sugarloaf Mountain in Chiricahua National Monument. Rhyolite formations such as Duck on a Rock along the Heart of Rocks Trail take longer to weather in the natural environments than the ever-changing sandstone formations found at Bryce's Canyon, Utah. The final chapter in volcanic history of the monument is the formation of dacite lava atop Sugarloaf Mountain. The dacite lava is the youngest volcanic rock found in the monument. Dacite is an erosion-resistant volcanic rock whose composition has qualities similar to basalt and rhyolite. Additional formations and rocks found in the Chiricahua Mountains include pillow lava, named such because it appears as a pillow seen around Onion Saddle. Solution pans, found in level areas throughout the Chiricahua National Monument, are dish-shaped depressions in rock formed by chemical and physical weathering. They hold rain, water and snowmelt in cavities several feet across and several inches deep. Slot canyons found along Echo Canyon Loop Trail formed as a result of freezing and thawing water in the cracks and crevices in the rocks, as well as by the forces of erosion and wind. Characterized as being forty times deeper than they are wide, the slot canyons are cut into the rhyolite rock formations.

A visit to the Chiricahua Mountains will also reveal sedimentary limestone and sandstone, both abundant in the northeastern corner of Chiricahua National Monument. These rocks are considered young, averaging 350 million years old. They date back to a time when southeastern Arizona was covered by an ancient sea. It is here where fossils can be found in the rocks, including brachiopods, gastropods and fossilized corals. Outside of the Chiricahua National Monument, scheelite-bearing limestone beds were discovered in 1945 only one thousand feet from the Galeyville town site. Scheelite contains defined tetragonal dipyramidal crystals similar to another Powellite. These crystals are evident when exposed by an ultraviolet lamp. Powellite fluoresces yellow, which indicates high molybdenum content. Scheelite fluoresces blue. More recent mining activity in the Galeyville area included tungsten extraction from scheelite deposits.

Escabrosa limestone composes the host rock of multiple cave sites in the Chiricahua Mountains. Stalactites and stalagmites are commonly found in these caves, having formed from the dripping deposits of water from the limestone ceiling. An example of a well-known cave in the Chiricahua Mountains is Crystal Cave, located behind Reed's Ranch. This limestone cavern and natural wonder was mined for crystals by Otto Duffner and his younger brother Max. Forest Supervisor Charles T. McGlone brought suit against the Duffners insisting that they cease operation. The cave was later heavily vandalized by visitors. By the mid-1970s, the entrance to crystal cave was locked up to prevent vandalism. A key can be obtained from the Portal Ranger Station to provide access. A network of tunnels leads to rooms and bottlenecks given descriptive names such as the Devil's Elbow and Fat Man's Misery. Flashlights and agility are necessary for visitation. The cave is also a popular area for the breeding of endangered bats, including the Mexican free-tailed species.

Located between San Bernardino Valley and San Simon Valley from the vantage point of the Chiricahua Mountains is the San Bernardino Volcanic Field, composed of 130 vents and cinder cones formed by small volcanoes between thirty thousand and one million years ago. It is around this area that there are many hot springs. Small explosion craters, such as Paramore Crater, created by steam blasts are also evident. Paramore Crater is composed of areas of olivine basalt with inclusions of obsidian. Derived from local volcanic activity in the San Bernardino Valley, the crater was named after James Harrison Parramore, who, along with his partner Claiborne Walker Merchant, established the San Simon Cattle and Canal Company, a ranch located in the San Simon Valley. The crater itself is located on a private ranch near the drainage divide between the San Simon Valley and the San Bernardino Valley. Oval-shaped Paramore

Looking over the rim of Paramore Crater. *Courtesy of Armando M. Arvizu.*

Crater is classified as a volcanic Maars crater, a coneless volcanic crater that has been formed by a single explosion and measures less than a mile in diameter and two hundred feet deep.

Southeastern Arizona is an area in the world where earthquakes are uncommon. An average of four or five have occurred in the region over the past 20,000 years with intervals in between of 3,500 years. Most earthquakes occur along plate boundaries that are present in the crust and mantle of the earth. On May 3, 1887, the 7.4-magnitude Pitaycachi Sonora earthquake was the largest historical earthquake recorded in southeastern Arizona. It was felt as far north as Phoenix, Arizona, and as far south as Mexico City. The earthquake, along with the fault, was the product of ongoing crustal extension—the same powerful forces that created the Basin and Range Province found in the western United States and northern Mexico. The epicenter of this earthquake was forty miles south of Douglas at Batepito, Sonora. It was located along the Pitaycachi fault, which encompassed thirty miles in the San Bernardino Valley in Sonora, Mexico. This fault is one of several that affects southeastern Arizona, southwestern New Mexico and Sonora, Mexico. The shaking resulting from the earthquake lasted five to ten minutes. The Mexican town of Bavispe was destroyed, and the earthquake caused several dozen deaths on both sides of the border, along with the destruction of a multitude of buildings. The earthquake resulted in rockslides as far as the Santa Catalina Mountains in Tucson, coupled with brush fires and forest fires in southeastern Arizona and northern Mexico. The valleys in southeastern Arizona, including Sulphur Springs and San Bernardino, were affected by shifts of water from underground, causing the displacement of natural springs and water flows. Despite the magnitude of the Pitaycachi earthquake, little damage was incurred on the balanced rock formations in Chiricahua National Monument. Rock slides and fires in the mountains around Rucker Canyon were some of the reported damages, along with several adobe buildings destroyed on John Slaughter's ranch.

Chapter 2

Mining

As with many localities in Arizona, miners viewed the Chiricahua Mountains as a potential mineral investment. Some sources claim that even the Apache chief Cochise had a secret gold mining operation on the Chiricahua Reservation during its brief existence in the early 1870s. By the end of the decade, the California mining district was established. The California mining district in the Chiricahua Mountains included several towns that developed over time and were the result of mining. Their longevity differed due to logistics and the market price of the metal that was being mined. They included the ephemeral Chiricahua City, followed by Galeyville and later the town of Paradise, which experienced its largest population growth, reaching three hundred by 1904. The rise and fall of Galeyville and Hilltop was connected to the market price of silver. The town of Portal, still in existence today, served as a gateway to the mining operations around Paradise.

Quartz outcroppings, an indicator of potential gold deposits discovered around Galeyville, enticed prospectors to follow the fault in search of precious metals. Metamorphosed Paleozoic country rock in the form of limestone found at the Hilltop Mine and around Galeyville served as replacement deposits for silver, lead, zinc and tungsten. These towns depended on the mineral wealth extracted from the local mines to operate. The payroll of the Chiricahua Mine supported the town of Paradise.

One of the most significant mineral-producing events that occurred in the American Southwest was the Laramide orogeny. It was this event that involved volcanism and faulting activity sixty-five million years ago that enabled the deposition of mineralized fluids that became the ores of gold, silver and copper. Many profitable ore-bearing regions in Arizona are the result of this event, including Bisbee, Globe/Miami, Morenci and Ray. While some areas resulted in high mineralization, others did not or have not yet been discovered. The Chiricahua Mountains are an example of the latter. Although mining was prevalent in parts of the Chiricahua Mountains in the late nineteenth and into parts of the twentieth century, it never was a truly profitable venture. Unlike the rich copper ore body discovered in Bisbee in the Mule Mountains southwest of the Chiricahua Mountains, for the most part, the Chiricahua Mountains contain weak mineralization. Mineral content in the Chiricahua Mountains includes lead oxides found near the surface encased in Paleozoic limestone. It also included marble deposits located in its northwest region that were mined during the early twentieth century.

The California mining district comprised the majority of land situated south of Apache Pass and north of Tex Canyon. It was formed on September 7, 1878, as a result of a meeting held at Leroy's Camp on Silver Creek by local miners declaring their adherence to the U.S. Mining Law of May 10, 1872. The arrival of the Southern Pacific Railroad at the old Butterfield Stage Station in San Simon on September 4, 1880, brought about heightened mining interest in the Chiricahua Mountains, which lay twenty-six miles south. The first recorded mining claim in the Chiricahua Mountains was the Hidden Treasure, worked by Jack Dunn in early 1881. It later became part of the Hilltop Mine. The area produced a high-grade ore that was handpicked and shipped by mule for processing to such railroad points as Willcox and Lordsburg. The California mining district continued to produce small amounts of ore into the 1980s with the El Tigre Mine (1941–82.) This locality produced 2,200–2,300 short tons of ore, including 11 ounces of gold, 2,662 ounces of silver and 73 pounds of copper. The El Tigre Mine host rock is composed of limestone, shale and volcanic rocks. The King of Lead Mine adjacent to the northeastern boundary of the Chiricahua National Monument was noted for its lead and zinc deposits. The King of Lead Mine—a lead, gold, zinc, copper and silver mine discovered in 1900 by John C. Riggs—was an active producer of metals through the early 1980s, with over 350 tons of ore processed. The total production for the California mining district between 1902 and 1954 included 28,000 short tons of ore, which equaled $1,072,000 with 176 short tons copper, 290 ounces of gold, 4,035 short tons of lead, 117,000 ounces of silver and 582 short tons of zinc.

The California mining district's history of production was over $1.75 million. However, when compared to the 8 billion pounds of copper extracted from the Warren mining district in Bisbee, it may be construed as less significant.

Founded on October 25, 1880, Chiricahua City was the first mining town established in the Chiricahua Mountains. Located near Portal Road north of the Galeyville town site, Chiricahua City was a popular site for early settlement in the Chiricahua Mountains due to its vast, open terrain, which was advantageous against the threat of Apache Indian attacks. Its flat geography made it conducive to scrupulous owners who wished to sell acreage to traveling pioneers from back east. The town's existence was short-lived. Its residents and businesses moved to Galeyville shortly after its creation because of Galeyville's access to well water, as well as its natural barrier against the elements and Indian attacks, along with shade and accessibility to mining claims.

Galeyville, unlike Chiricahua City, lasted longer and was both renowned and infamous, according to historians. Galeyville has historically been given a reputation as a town run by outlaws during its existence; it was the silver-boom potential that allowed for the town's establishment and livelihood. Outlaws such as Curly Bill Brocius and Johnny Ringo were known to frequent the town as a break from cattle rustling. However, after the Apache Indian chief Loco's raid on April 26, 1882, the locals of Galeyville lost faith in the outlaw element's ability to defend the town. The outlaws chose to flee the town rather than face the onslaught of the Apache raid. Jeptha Bennett Ayers, a saloonkeeper from the mining town of Charleston, and Charles C. Clute established the Chiricahua Mining & Milling Company. Owning several claims in Pinery Canyon near Galeyville, the company built a thirty-ton Rankin-Brayton smelter that processed ore primarily from the Dunn Mine. Their mine was known as Ayers Camp, later known as the Hilltop Mine, which included a combination of mining and smelter operators. In the spring of 1882, Apache raids on the camp that consisted of burning and looting ultimately led to its destruction, with the inhabitants retreating to Willcox or Galeyville.

Despite many recorded hostilities between cattle rustlers and lawmen, there were times when an amicable relationship existed. One such occasion involved Cochise County deputy sheriff William M. Breakenridge. On a business trip to Galeyville in May 1881, the presence of the lawman aroused the hostility of Curly Bill Brocius's colleague in crime by the name of Wallace. Wallace's threatening of Brocius's friend Breakenridge angered Curly Bill, who later had a shootout with Wallace. Wallace ended up shooting Curly Bill through the right side of the neck. Curly Bill never did prosecute Wallace for his actions. The relationship between Deputy Sheriff Breakenridge and Curly Bill was not the only example of an amicable relationship between the law and the outlaws. Breakenridge described an incident in which he commandeered Curly Bill to assist him in rounding up delinquent taxes from local cattlemen in the Chiricahua Mountains. He also elaborated on poker games that occurred in Tombstone among the Earp brothers, Johnny Ringo and Curly Bill.

The claims of high mineral content in the mines around Galeyville were sensationalized by its namesake, John H. Galey, a pioneer oilman from Pennsylvania, and other promoters to lure investors and mining interests. The first mining claim near Galeyville was the Texas Mine in October 29, 1879. Galeyville began as a silver-mining camp in the fall of 1880. It grew rapidly, encompassing over five thousand people in a matter of several weeks. Ten saloons, two butcher shops and six general stores, along with a barbershop and a Wells Fargo office, are some of the businesses that operated out of Galeyville. Many mining claims followed, yet few produced or developed around Galeyville. A smelter was installed at Galeyville for processing the ore extracted from nearby mines. It was made by and transported from the Pacific Iron Works in San Francisco. The smelter operated at a thirty-ton-per-week capacity. Due to Galeyville's brief existence and low slag count (three hundred tons), it probably operated for several months before being dismantled and shipped elsewhere. The Campbell Mill near the Texas Mine in Galeyville consisted of a two-stamp mill used to crush ore.

The town of Galeyville met a slow demise between 1880 and 1896, when it held its last election. Factors that caused the demise of Galeyville included the following: the insolvency of its founder, John H. Galey, who was in debt with his Galeyville investments for the amount of $180,000; the severe drought in 1882 affecting the dependable supply of water at Turkey Creek, despite the fact that some inhabitants with wells managed to sustain themselves through the dry period; and the raids of the Apache Indian chief Loco on Galeyville, along with those of Geronimo and other Apache, made the region less desirable to local inhabitants. On one occasion, six troops of cavalry were dispatched against the raiders, who met their opponent in a firefight at Horseshoe Canyon on April 22, 1882. The Apache escaped, taking losses of two, while the cavalry had six men dead and four wounded. On April 24, 1882, the raiders were again on the warpath, killing Deputy Sheriff Hugh Goodman in the vicinity of Galeyville. Although no deaths occurred in Galeyville, sensationalism among its inhabitants led to the claim that thirty-five people were wantonly slaughtered in Galeyville by Apache in a headline known as the Galeyville massacre. Because of suspicion of its use as a base for harboring cattle rustlers in the form of squatters, the town was targeted for the removal of people and buildings by the San Simon Cattle Company in 1888. Perhaps the final blow to the integrity of the town was the demonetizing of silver that was authorized by the U.S. government in 1893. This action negatively impacted the local mining operations for which the town was originally established.

The Hilltop Mine was the largest mine in the Chiricahua Mountains. It was also the most profitable and well-known mine in the Chiricahua Mountains. Located on the northwest slope of Shaw Peak, the mine operated in the 1880s as Ayers Camp under the ownership of Jack Dunn. It was worked for rich oxide lead silver ore near the surface. It consisted of three interconnected levels encompassing 20,007 feet. Several of the tunnels were named after prominent stockholders. Several miles of workings, including the creation of tunnels such as the Kasper Tunnel, were developed between the 1880s and the late 1920s. Ore was hand-sorted and shipped originally by mules and later by heavy-duty trucks to the railroad in Rodeo en route to Willcox, Arizona, or Lordsburg,

Seen here is a distant view of the Kasper Tunnel at the Hilltop Mine. The Hilltop Metal Mining Company employed an average of forty men during the 1920s. The Hilltop Metal Mining Company ceased operation in 1927. The period of greatest development for the Hilltop Mine was from 1924 to 1926, when 11,373 short tons of ore yielding five million pounds of lead and 57,600 ounces of silver were mined. The greatest amount of ore came from the Kasper and Grey levels of the Hilltop Mine. Low metal prices and depleted ore reserves caused the mine to close in 1929. Little production took place over the next twenty years. The mine was worked intermittently since the early 1950s. *Courtesy of William Ascarza.*

A scene depicted inside the Kasper Tunnel. Between 1902 and 1950, 28,700 tons of ore and concentrates valued at $1.1 million was extracted from the Hilltop Mine. These included 290 ounces of gold, 117,000 ounces of silver, 4,035 tons of lead, 582 tons of zinc and 176 tons of copper. The Hilltop Mine included five miles of tunnels and a variety of minerals including cerrusite, galena, jarosite, pyrite, scheelite, smithsonite and wulfenite. *Courtesy of William Ascarza.*

New Mexico, then on to the smelter in El Paso, Texas. Some of the ore at the Blacksmith level of the Hilltop Mine was milled at the town of Paradise.

Frank and John Hands acquired the Hilltop Mine in the 1890s. The copper, lead, silver and zinc ores proved profitable, allowing them to invest in the mining equipment necessary for extraction. The Hands brothers were responsible for building many of the trails connecting the mines around Hilltop. In 1913, they sold their interest to the Hilltop Metal Mining Company for $120,000, which was both a large sum of money back in those days and the largest recorded profit made in the history of mining operations in the Chiricahua Mountains at the time.

The town of Hilltop owed its existence to the nearby Hilltop Mine. It was located on the east slope of the Chiricahua Mountains on two sides of 7,700-foot-tall Shaw Peak, accessible through the Kasper Tunnel workings. The main tunnel was above several levels below it whose entrance originated from Whitetail Canyon on the eastside of the mountain. The ore was mined and transported through winzes and vertical shafts, eventually dropped down to the lowest tunnel and then transported to the surface by mule-drawn carts. The town of Hilltop included an assortment of miners' bunkhouses, billiard halls, restaurants and manager's quarters. Some of these structures remain to this day, although they are on private land. All that remains of the western slope of Hilltop are several concrete structures and abundant mine tailings from the Kasper Tunnel entrance. Although the town of Hilltop reported one hundred people in 1930, its population would decline in the following year due to the inactivity of the mine. The post office was active from January 26, 1920, until June 20, 1945.

Other than gold, one of the most sought-after minerals in the Chiricahua Mountains is the wulfenite that was extracted in a stope at the Hilltop Mine. Wulfenite is a lead molybdate that is noted for its tabular crystals that are in the shape of squares. Colors of wulfenite vary throughout Arizona from brilliant red, orange and yellow to gray, brown or greenish brown. The physical appearance of wulfenite found at the Hilltop Mine is thickly bladed, taking on a distinct butterscotch color, in contrast to wulfenite found in other localities in Arizona. The distinct appearance of Hilltop Mine wulfenite is both lustrous and translucent with crystals over a quarter inch in size mixed with a calcite matrix. Large cabinet specimens of wulfenite from the Hilltop Mine are uncommon. From 1890 through World War I, wulfenite was extracted from the Hilltop Mine. Some of this wulfenite that was collected ended up in museums. Prices for specimens range in the hundreds to thousands of dollars, depending on their size and crystal quality.

On the author's first journey to the Hilltop Mine, he had the rare opportunity of meeting a border patrol agent in the field of duty who needed to view imagery taken from one of his field cameras. The author had his laptop available, and conversation ensued discussing the effects of the Horseshoe 2 Fire the previous summer. On that occasion, the author was trying to find the unmarked Northfork Road to the Hilltop Mine. After the agent was granted the use of the author's laptop to view imagery of illegal immigrants roaming the periphery near Pinery Canyon Road, the author was given a description of the Northfork Road.

The town of Paradise was named for the available water in nearby Turkey Creek since the area was deemed a paradise surrounded by arid landscape. Some sources claim it was named by a local mining family so awed by its presence and beauty that they called the area "Paradise." Another possibility is that the name was derived from ore teamsters who called the place "Paradise" because of the availability of water for their animals. In its prime in 1901, the town included thirteen saloons, several general stores and a two-story hotel. During its brief existence, the jail consisted of the great outdoors. Prisoners were chained to two trees.

A fine specimen of wulfenite from the Hilltop Mine seen here is currently on display at the Flandrau Mineral Museum at the University of Arizona. *Courtesy of William Ascarza.*

The Duffner brothers are considered the founders of Portal. Portal's post office opened in 1905 and remains active. Located at the north of Cave Creek Canyon, Portal was named by Oregon miner Jack Thomas. The name was derived from the fact that the post office was at the entrance of Cave Creek Canyon. Portal was to become a mining suburb of Paradise and its surrounding mines. Those mines were expected to produce abundant mineral wealth on the level of Bisbee and Butte. The Chiricahua Mine was Paradise's largest mining operation. The Chiricahua Mine was worked heavily in the early 1900s by the Lake Superior Mining Company, although none of the ore was shipped, and the profits, if any, were marginal. The mine consisted of several levels connected by a 480-foot shaft. The financial panic of 1907, caused by over-speculation in banking, mining and railroad stock, caused metal prices to plummet across the country and the closure of many mines.

Arizona was rated one of the top five producers of architectural marble in the United States in the early twentieth century. Located near Fort Bowie in MacIntosh Canyon (sometimes known as Marble Canyon), a marble mining operation was established in 1909 after positive exploration undertaken by the Arizona Geological Survey the previous year. John G.

The mining town of Paradise in the heart of the Chiricahua Mountains as seen in 1914. *Courtesy of* Mining Science.

Kerr, a representative for the Arizona Marble Company, based in Colorado, deemed the property an important asset with rich marble deposits. He considered it worthy of an investment, including the establishment of an access road from the quarry site to the Southern Pacific Railroad, fourteen miles north at Olga Station near the town of Bowie. This would allow for the accessibility of ore shipments. It would include the erection of bridges, a necessity when traversing the natural features of the rugged landscape, such as the canyons and massive gorge, the size of which called for the use of rail trestles emplaced with concrete and pine timbers.

The company supplied high-grade marble to builders in cities throughout the United States, including Denver, Colorado; Missoula, Montana; and Champaign, Illinois. Banks and churches were some of the buildings constructed using marble from this locality in the northwestern part of the Chiricahua Mountains. The marble blocks from the quarry measured over six feet high and were highly sought after because of their colors, which included black, blue, green, white and rose-colored veins. At sixty tons per load when placed in wagons, the blocks were moved by 110-horsepower steam engines.

Marble is defined as a limestone or dolomite that has been naturally heated (metamorphosed) and recrystallized. Marble mining required a skill set to preserve the final product. The miners were limited in their ability to use explosives for fear that it would damage the rock. They relied on the use of steam-powered drills, saws and derricks to cut, shape and hoist the material before it was transported out of the quarry. The two derricks that operated at the site were rated for thirty and fifty tons. The Arizona Marble Company relied on equipment provided by the Sullivan Machinery Company to aid in the marble extraction operation.

The marble quarry, pit and machinery seen here was operated by the Arizona Marble Company around 1911. It was the job of two 115-horsepower water tube boilers to supply the necessary steam for operating the rock drills in the quarry. The block of marble the man is seen standing on was not larger than twelve feet long containing two hundred cubic feet. *Courtesy of Fort Bowie National Historic Site.*

A view of the camp buildings near the marble quarry. *Courtesy of Fort Bowie National Historic Site.*

Financed by a group of Denver investors, a steam-powered mill was developed at the site that aided in hoisting, sizing and cutting the slabs of marble. It also pumped water from four constructed wells and was fueled by native vegetation, including juniper and oak trees. As those sources diminished, coal was substituted, having been imported from New Mexico. A machine shop, along with a blacksmith shop, serviced the operation, with the miners living in a tent camp several hundred feet away.

Today, all that remains of the original quarry operation are boilers, cables, heavy-duty wheels, milling equipment, concrete piers and wooden derricks, along with a water pump engraved "Fairbanks Morse." Visitors to the quarry site are impressed with the massive size of the marble blocks that measure over six feet in height. They attest to the skill and labor that went into this mining enterprise. Despite its short-lived operation ending a century ago, marble is still quarried at a nearby site in the Dos Cabezas Mountains.

Chapter 3

Apache

The Apache Indians would play an important role in the history and permanent settlement in the Chiricahua Mountains. The Chiricahua Apache were known as the "Cherrycows" among the pioneers who settled the mountain range. Their presence was commanding, and their raids on the Spanish, Mexican and, later, American settlers proved legendary, provocative and deadly. However, their forces fought piecemeal against the more homogenous forces of the U.S. Army. Because of this and their limited numbers, they could only fight delaying actions against the inevitable taming of the American Southwest by the U.S. military. As a mountain-dwelling people, the Apache were skilled raiders who used guerrilla warfare tactics with such finesse that they could hinder and distract U.S. troop movement in the Southwest. Some later served as scouts for the U.S. Army. Ultimately, however, their presence in the Southwest proved a hindrance to the expansion of the United States' interests, which including mining, ranching, farming and settlement. It was their fate to be forcibly removed and forever vanquished from their native lands.

The Apache hailed from Asia, arriving in North America around 1000 BC. A nomadic people, they eventually migrated south from Canada into what is known today as southeastern Arizona, southwestern New Mexico and the Sierra Madre mountains in northern Mexico. It was in the Chiricahua Mountains that the Apache used as a base for raiding operations, probably because of the natural fortification of the rock formations. The pinnacles of rocks were called "standing up rock" by the Chiricahua Apache. The Apache also referred to the Chiricahua Mountains as the "Land of Standing-Up Rocks."

Consisting of bands located in Arizona, New Mexico and northern Mexico, the Apache were not a unified tribe. Several bands of Apache present in the Chiricahua Mountains included the Eastern Chiricahuas (Chihenne), who inhabited the Black Mountains region of southwestern New Mexico; the Central Chiricahuas (Chokonen), who inhabited the mountains of southeastern Arizona; the Southern Chiricahuas (Nednhi), who lived in the Sierra Madre Mountains of northern Sonora, Mexico; and the Bedonkohe. The latter two bands were assimilated into the former two bands by the 1880s because their numbers were severely reduced by encounters with the United States and Mexican militaries.

Warfare was routine for the Apache, who hindered settlement of the Spanish, Mexicans and Americans from the late 1600s into the 1930s. They were well established in the Chiricahua Mountains by the time the Spanish arrived in the seventeenth century. Spanish land claims to Indian lands were by virtue of discovery. Spain officially declared war on the Apache in 1748.

Their methods of warfare were brutal. The Apache never scalped their victims; instead, they crushed their heads with rocks to prevent the dead from recognizing them in the afterlife. The term *Apache* may have derived from *Apachu*, the Zuni Indian word for "enemy." Apache were also known as Ndee or Dine'e, meaning "the people." Although the Apache were well known as raiders, they were also hunters and gatherers. The Chiricahua Apache preferred to hunt wild game, including deer, rabbits and turkey. Crops included pumpkins, melons, beans and corn, and the latter was used to make tizwin, a weak beer. Agave, also known as century plant, was used to make mescal, a distilled alcoholic beverage.

Both Mexicans in the 1820s and, later, the U.S. Army beginning in the 1850s fought Apache in Arizona after acquiring the territory as a result of the Gadsden Purchase of 1853. The discovery of gold in the Pinos Altos region of southwestern New Mexico brought about early clashes between American miners and the Apache. The Butterfield Stage Station, built in the late 1850s, was visited by Apache who would trade wood and other necessary items. The Butterfield Overland Trail mapped through Apache Pass an area that would become the focal point of the Bascom Affair, a singular event that would instigate what became known as the Apache Wars, which would continue officially until 1886. As a result, settlement in and around the Chiricahua Mountains would remain perilous and not without casualties.

On January 29, 1861, the Apache Wars ignited due to an event known as the Bascom Affair. Occurring at Apache Pass, located north of the Chiricahua

Mountains, this event was named after Lieutenant George N. Bascom. The story begins with a twelve-year-old boy by the name of Felix Ward, who disappeared from a ranch owned by his stepfather, John Ward, and his common-law wife, Carmen Martinez. Second Lieutenant George Bascom, ordered by his commanding officer Lieutenant Colonel Pitcairn Morrison to pursue the Apache to recover the missing boy and stock stolen from a nearby ranch, was assigned fifty-four mounted troopers of Company C, Seventh U.S. Infantry. This singular event, along with the later execution of Apache Indian chief Mangas Coloradas, would have far-reaching consequences for the future relationship between the United States and the Chiricahua Apache over the course of the next twenty-five years. Mangas Coloradas, meaning "red sleeves" in Spanish, was aptly named for his habit of wearing a red shirt.

Bascom was not a seasoned officer, and his actions over the next several weeks would prove his shortcomings. He informed the employees at the Butterfield Stagecoach Station at Apache Pass of his intention to meet Cochise, one of the more prominent Apache chiefs. Although he was loath toward Mexicans, Cochise was not at first antagonistic toward the arrival of the American settlers. However, he did have suspicions that proved justifiable that his home territory was in jeopardy. The massive influx of Americans backed by the United States military did much to escalate tensions between the two parties.

Cochise and several of his family members met Bascom over dinner. Despite Cochise's repeated denial, Bascom accused Cochise of kidnapping the boy and placed him and his family under house arrest. Cochise slashed the tent in which he was confined with a knife, making an escape up a hill with soldiers firing at him. The phrase "Cut the Tent" originated from the Chiricahua Apache chief Cochise's reaction to being taken prisoner and having to cut his way out of a tent to escape arrest. However, several family members may have been injured or killed during the affair. Cochise attempted to get his family members returned under a flag of truce but was denied by Bascom, who demanded the boy, though Cochise claimed again that he did not have him.

Cochise's men attacked a wagon train along the Overland Trail, killing the Mexicans and taking Anglos hostage, including a Butterfield Stage Coach employee. Cochise thought he could conduct a prisoner swap, which was an accepted practice between the Apache and Mexicans. Again Bascom refused to comply with Cochise's negotiation tactics. Cochise tortured and killed the Anglo hostages in revenge. Though his wife and son were released, other male Apache were subsequently hanged by U.S. soldiers. Upon the grisly discovery of the bodies by the Chiricahua Apache, Cochise was so incensed by the actions of the U.S. army that he waged war against all military personnel, miners and settlers. During the War Between the States (1861–65), a large contingent of the U.S. military was fighting the Confederacy back east, leaving the Southwest to the mercy of the Apache.

The father-in-law to Cochise, Mangas Coloradas commanded 150 warriors against the Union soldiers in the two-day battle of Apache Pass on July 15 and 16, 1862, as they pursued the Confederates in New Mexico. Established on July 28, 1862, Fort Bowie was created as a result of the Battle of Apache Pass and the outcome of the Bascom Affair. Its purpose was to protect travelers against Apache deprivations in Apache Pass. It also provided the U.S. military with a base of operations from which to pursue the raiding Chiricahua Apache. In January 1863, Mangas Coloradas met with the American military's California Volunteers under a flag of truce and was subsequently executed. This unpardonable offense further raised the ire of Cochise and led to extensive hostilities between the Apache and American forces. After the death of Mangas Coloradas, the dual Apache chiefs Loco and Victorio assumed a more prominent role in the leadership of the Apache in the Southwest and would later become known for their raids against settlements in Arizona and New Mexico.

The central characters involved in the Bascom Affair met different fates. Lieutenant Bascom was promoted to captain and died at the Battle of Valverde, New Mexico. Originally buried at Fort Craig and later reinterred at Santa Fe, his remains were marked unknown. Felix, the boy whose disappearance started the Bascom Affair, was never recovered, and he spent the remainder of his formative years with the Western White Mountain Apache. However, he reappeared several decades later as an Indian scout by the name of Mickey Free. Cochise was a war leader and a man of honor. He excelled at planning and carrying out raids on settlers. Some historical accounts support the notion that he was involved in raids on the American settlers prior to the Bascom Affair. The Bascom Affair enhanced his standing from being a war leader in a local group within the Chiricahua tribe to a respected chieftain throughout the tribe and a force to be reckoned with both as warrior and a negotiator. Both Cochise and his father-in-law, Mangas Coloradas, had influence and power to unite an otherwise divided people against the encroachment of United States military and settlers. Cochise eventually made peace with the U.S. government in 1872. He died in 1874 and was buried in a secret grave site at Cochise Stronghold in the Dragoon Mountains west of the Chiricahua Mountains. Cochise County, established in his honor along with the railroad station also by that name, was named after the Apache chief.

The Battle Flag of the Confederacy waves proudly denoting the graves of four fallen Confederate soldiers belonging to a small company under the command of Captain Sherod Hunter. These soldiers en route to Texas were ambushed by Apache at the Butterfield Stage Coach Station in the Dragoon Mountains, twenty-five miles northeast of the Chiricahua Mountains, on May 5, 1862. Regardless of which side one was on during the War Between the States, the Apache cared not. *Courtesy of William Ascarza.*

In the 1860s, the Apache were on a rampage. Several major battles between the U.S. Army and the Apache occurred in the Chiricahua Mountains. One significant event that occurred on October 20, 1869, became known as the Campaign of the Rocky Mesa. It began with an Apache attack on a westbound stagecoach under military escort in the Dragoon Mountains, thirty miles west of the Chiricahua Mountains, on October 5 of the same year. All four soldiers, the driver and renowned Tucson miner Colonel John Finkle Stone (after whom Stone Avenue was later named) were killed. Hours after the ambush, the Apache struck again, this time against a group of cowboys in the Sulphur Springs Valley. One cowboy was killed, while another was fortunate to escape with his life to Fort Bowie. Two hundred cattle were confiscated by the Apache. A cavalry expedition was mounted from Fort Bowie under the command of Lieutenant William H. Winters in response to the Apache aggression. They pursued the forces of Cochise to one of his strongholds between Red Rock and Turtle Mountain above Rucker Canyon. There, a limited engagement known as the Campaign of the Rocky Mesa occurred. The battle fought in the Chiricahua Mountains involved the First and Eighth Cavalry, who successfully held off a band of attacking Apache forces. Sergeant Frederick Jarvis and Private Edward Pengally were among thirty-two cavalrymen that day cited for gallantry in action.

During the War Between the States, the U.S. Army under General Carleton carried out a policy of extermination of the Apache in Arizona. By 1868, there was a prevailing movement in the United States to make peace with the Indian tribes in the American West, including the Navajo, Shoshone and Sioux and eventually the Apache.

A peace treaty in October 1872 was arranged between Cochise and General Oliver O. Howard at a place known today as Cochise Council Rock, located in the western foothills among the large balanced rocks in the Dragoon Mountains. Thomas J. Jeffords served as the agent for the 1,244 Apache on the newly created Chiricahua Indian Reservation. The reservation would remain autonomous from the nearby U.S. presence at Fort Bowie for less than four years. During that time, the reservation headquarters was moved three times—from the Sulphur Spring Valley to the San Simon Cienega and finally to Turkey Creek in the west side of the Chiricahua Mountains. The reason for these moves was to avoid the spread of malaria and conflicts with the white peddlers of contraband arms and liquor.

In 1874, authority over the Arizona reservations was transferred from the U.S. War Department to the Indian Bureau. This action would have a far-reaching effect. It was through the Indian Bureau that a plan was initiated to transfer all of the Apache Bands to the San Carlos Indian Reservation. This plan was objected to by General George Crook, who had assumed command from General Stoneman of the Military Department of Arizona in 1871. General Crook recognized each band's distinct ethnographic differences. It was General George Crook's winter campaign of 1872–73 that effectively ended the Indian Wars in north-central Arizona.

Apache raids continued in southern Arizona after the peace made between Cochise and General Howard. In 1873, a California-bound family by the name of Harris was ambushed by the Apache under the command of Juh, who was known for leading several raiding parties against settlements in southeastern Arizona. Juh was an Apache leader who instigated the uprising at the San Carlos Indian Reservation in the early 1880s. Most family members, including Harris, his wife and two children, were killed. His fifteen-year-old daughter was taken prisoner by the Apache and rescued by the Second Cavalry in 1876. A grave marker denoting the experience is located in the east side of the Chiricahua Mountains, four miles north of Paradise. General Crook provided a military show of force in 1874 that temporarily halted Apache raids and placed the majority of Apache on the reservations. Afterward, Crook was transferred to fight Indians in the Northern Plains. However, he would return to Arizona a decade later to contend with the raids of Geronimo.

Following Cochise's death in 1874, the Chiricahua Apache lacked a central tribal chief since both Cochise's sons, Taza and Nachez, were not themselves natural leaders. The responsibility was taken on by Juh, Noglee and, later, Geronimo, a former medicine man turned guerrilla leader who was successful in instigating one of the United States' largest military operations against Indians in the western states. Geronimo was known among his band as *Goyahkla*, meaning "man who is clever" or "the man who yawns." The name "Geronimo" is derived from Jerome or St. Jerome, to whom the Mexicans called out during an Apache raid.

The Chiricahua Indian Reservation was short-lived, lasting from 1872 to 1876. Several reasons for this included the discovery of gold in the White Mountains and the additional mineral discoveries in the Dragoon Mountains and Chiricahua Mountains, which further convinced the U.S. government to remove the Apache from those areas and consolidate them at the San Carlos Indian Reservation. There was also an interest among ranchers to acquire land set aside as Indian reservations because the land contained plentiful grasses for raising cattle. The pivotal event that culminated in the closure of the Chiricahua Indian Reservation was the wanton killing of several stagecoach employees. Nicholas M. Rogers, a Missourian, along with his employee O.O. Spence, operated the Overland Mail Stage Station in the Sulphur Spring Valley. They provided whiskey and mescal to travelers, as well as Apache on the reservation. However, on April 7, 1876, Rogers was killed by an Apache to whom he had refused to provide whiskey. Spence was also killed. The Apache then took to raiding neighboring settlements in both the San Pedro and Sulphur Spring Valleys. This ended the peace between the United States and the Apache. Indian Agent Tom Jeffords was subsequently replaced by John Clum.

Anson P.K. Safford, the territorial governor of Arizona, petitioned for the removal of the Apache from the Chiricahua Indian Reservation because of their proximity to the Mexican border. President Grant signed an executive order in response to the uprising that transferred all the Chiricahua Apache to the San Carlos Indian Reservation east of Globe, Arizona. As a result, the Chiricahua Indian Reservation became public domain on October 30, 1876. The closure of the Chiricahua Indian Reservation allowed an influx of ranchers to acquire land around the Chiricahua Mountains. However, it heightened Apache aggression in Arizona, New Mexico and also the settlements across the border in Mexico. The grasslands of southeastern Arizona were ripe for the taking. A decade of instability followed that continued until Geronimo's surrender in September 1886.

The Chiricahua Apache abhorred the San Carlos Indian Reservation. Several reasons for their disdain for the reservation included the concern of the spread of malaria on the reservation, a distrust of the United States military and the potential of living a free life in the Sierra Madre Mountains of Mexico. The San Carlos Indian Reservation lacked the forests and elevation to which they were accustomed. Malaria outbreaks at the San Carlos Indian Reservation between the years 1878 and 1880 claimed 150 Apache. By 1880, 700 Apache lived on the San Carlos Indian Reservation. Problems regarding assimilation again prevented peace between the United States military and the Apache. The traditional Apache economy was based heavily on raiding and warfare, combined with hunting and gathering edible plants. Farming on the reservation was not their specialty. Additional reasons for the resumption of Chiricahua Apache hostilities in southeastern Arizona included the prohibition of tizwin, a favorite alcoholic beverage, on the reservation.

The Apache on the San Carlos Indian Reservation, including Naiche and Mangas, sons of Cochise and Mangas Coloradas, broke out of the reservation on several occurrences. Victorio, a leader of the Eastern Chiricahua, fled from the San Carlos Reservation in 1877 with 350 men, women and children, along with a herd of stolen horses. The group returned to New Mexico and managed to maintain a quiet presence on their homeland for a year before conflict rose again when the U.S. Department of the Interior ordered them back to the San Carlos Indian Reservation. Preferring to resist, Victorio headed for the mountains with 50 men and conducted a series of raids in the Rio Grande Valley. The U.S. Department of the Interior made a change in policy, recommending that Victorio's band be sent to the Mescalero Indian Reservation, located east of the Rio Grande. However, local authorities in New Mexico considered his forces a threat to settlement because of the mass killings and damages caused by the raids of Victorio's band, which had grown in recruits to 200 men. By 1880, Victorio's raiding forces had killed over 1,000 people and had evaded U.S and Mexican military forces numbering in the thousands. Victorio's superb tactics and ability to live off the land made him feared as a powerful force. However, he relied on ammunition acquired from both raids and fallen U.S. and Mexican soldiers.

On October 14, 1880, Victorio's ammunition shortage became crucial, and his forces were cut off from the mountains in Mexico. He was subsequently surrounded by the Mexican army and executed.

Geronimo would escape with his brother-in-law Juh from the San Carlos Indian Reservation in April 1878. Capturing a wagon train of guns and ammunition, they journeyed south to the Sierra Madre Mountains in northern Mexico. They attempted to entice Loco and his band to join them, making several returns to the San Carlos Indian Reservation. The Apache were a restless and divided group, not content to remain in the safe confines of the relatively inaccessible Sierra Madres. They also contended with temptation toward raids into Arizona and Mexico, which further aroused the militaries of the United States and Mexico. It was the local raids in southeastern Arizona that really put communities on edge regarding the Apache threat. The early 1880s witnessed many such raids resulting in the theft and destruction of property and wanton killing of locals. The Chiricahua Mountains were one of the targets of multiple raids led by Apache forces riding north from Mexico. Loco and his band of Chiricahua Apache (150 or so) ravaged the northeastern Chiricahua Mountains. The battle in Horseshoe Canyon, ten miles southeast of Galeyville, in 1882 bears testament to the malevolent action of the Apache. According to the April 26, 1882 edition of the *Tombstone Epitaph*, this raid led to the pillage and attack on Galeyville by Loco and his followers that caused the death of thirty-five settlers. Other reports also listed the death of a deputy sheriff.

Some of the famous Chiricahua Apache raids from Mexico into southeastern Arizona included Nana's raid in 1881 followed by the raids of Geronimo and Naiche at the San Carlos Indian Reservation the following year. Additional raids included the raids of Chato and Bonito, along with the raids of Geronimo and Ulzana, as well as Naiche's raid at Fort Apache in May 1886. In these raids, the Apache were trying to replenish guns, horses and ammunition. It was Chato's raid in the spring of 1883 that prompted General Crook to pursue the Apache across the international border. Crook had several hundred men in his force to carry out the pursuit, over half of whom were Apache scouts. He was successful in convincing the renegade Apache to return to the San Carlos Indian Reservation. This included over four hundred Apache, along with leaders Geronimo, Chato, Naiche and Chihuahua. Josanie led a raid in August 1885 near Galeyville, killing John Keating, a local Galeyville resident and rancher, along with Casper Albert, a local miner. They journeyed four miles north of White Tail Canyon, stealing a prime herd of horses. Afterward, they headed down south across the border to Mexico. This was followed by Ulzana's November raid that killed thirty-eight people and stole 250 horses. This raid encompassed a 1,200-mile stretch of territory, including the Chiricahua Mountains down into Mexico.

The return of General Crook from the northern Great Plains to the Southwest in 1882 brought about reforms in the San Carlos Indian Reservation and the military. He expelled squatters and trespassers from the reservation while improving its administration and also offered additional financial incentives to entice the Indians to farm. General Crook's largest contribution to the field of Indian fighting was to use Apache scouts to track renegade Apache. His goal was to bring Geronimo and his group of renegade Apache back to the reservation. A major agreement between the United States and Mexican president Porfirio Diaz in July 29, 1882, allowed U.S. forces to cross the border in pursuit of Apache and follow them to their mountain enclaves. This would serve him well the following year when he advanced a force of fifty soldiers and two hundred scouts to flush out the raiding parties of Chato and Benito in the Sierra Madre, ultimately leading to one of Geronimo's early surrenders in March 1884.

Peace reigned for a year due to attempts by the United States to pacify the Apache, including Geronimo, by interesting them in crop cultivation and through the firm hand of Captain Emmet Crawford, in charge of the San Carlos Indian Reservation. However, discontent occurred at the reservation due to General Crook's ban on both tizwin and wife beating. Geronimo and a party of forty-two men and ninety-two women and children escaped the reservation for Mexico. Apache raids began to ignite again. It was in the vicinity of Cave Creek Canyon that on September 29, 1885, an unidentified prospector was killed by Apache forces under the command of the Apache leader Chihuahua, who, the following day, raided the Keating Ranch, stealing horses and killing Michael Keating. General Crook initiated another Sierra Madre campaign to capture Geronimo and his forces. This long and arduous campaign initially succeeded in convincing Geronimo to surrender at Canyon de los Embudos, twelve miles south of the border, on March 25, 1886. However, Tribolet, a French trader, got Geronimo and his band of twenty followers drunk. As a result, they fled for the hills rather than surrender. General Crook resigned as a result over mounting criticism of his Apache campaign. General Philip Sheridan replaced Crook with General Nelson A. Miles. Miles was given five thousand enlisted men, a full 25 percent of the entire U.S. Army, with which to subdue and capture Geronimo and his small party, estimated around forty, with only sixteen of them warriors.

General Miles was an ardent supporter of using heliograph stations for linking military bases in the Southwest. Many in southeastern Arizona were on mountain ranges, including the Chiricahua Mountains and the nearby Swisshelm Mountains. General Miles's mission was two-fold. He had to capture Geronimo while protecting settlers in Arizona and New Mexico. Miles concluded the Apache Wars by implementing two major policies. The first was deporting the majority of the Chiricahua Apache to Fort Marion, Florida, whether they were hostile, peaceful, residing on or off the reservation or in the service as Apache scouts for the U.S. Army. The reasoning was that they could not supply arms and food to the renegade Apache. The second was to offer a peace plan where Geronimo's forces were to be sent to Florida. Miles was fortunate to have the services of Lieutenant Charles B. Gatewood, a seasoned veteran of Crook's Apache campaign, who was proficient in the Apache dialect. It was Gatewood, along with several Apache scouts, who convinced Geronimo to surrender his forces, which averaged around thirty-five in number, to General Miles at Skeleton Canyon on September 4, 1886.

Geronimo, pictured here, was a medicine man turned guerrilla fighter. Unlike Cochise, Mangas, Victorio and Juh, who truly were major leaders in the Apache Wars, Geronimo's actions may have been embellished, since his force numbered fewer than fifty men. He has the honor of having instigated the largest United States military manhunt (roughly five thousand enlisted men) in the history of the Indian Wars in the Southwest. His force managed to elude capture by General Crook and General Miles until September 4, 1886. *Courtesy of Library of Congress Prints and Photographs Division.*

Many of the Chiricahua Apache imprisoned at Fort

Heliograph stations were versatile as well as portable, using rays of sunlight that reflected off a mirror up to forty miles in any direction to report movement of Apache. Shutters interrupted the beams of light, allowing for the transmission of dots and dashes of Morse code. The transmissions were received and read by troops at different stations, including Fort Bowie. Relays from these points were then sent to Fort Huachuca and Fort Bayard, New Mexico. Communication could also be established as far away as Fort Lowell in Tucson. *Courtesy of the National Archives & Records Administration.*

A surrender conference is taking place between General Crook and Geronimo at Canyon de los Embudos on March 25, 1886. *From left to right*: Lieutenant William F. Shipp, Captain C.S. Roberts, Geronimo, Concepcion, Nana, Noche, Lieutenant Marion P. Maus, Jose Maria, Antonia Besias, Jose Montoyo, Captain John Gregory Bourke, General Crook and Charlie Roberts. *Courtesy of* Scenes in Geronimo's Camp, *published by Mary Fly, 1905.*

Apache and the U.S. military at Fort Bowie prior to their departure to Florida. *Courtesy of Fort Bowie National Historic Site.*

Marion perished from the elements. They were transferred from that locality to Alabama and then to Fort Sill, Oklahoma. It was not until August 1912 that Congress removed their prisoner of war status. After their release, the majority of the remaining 250 Apache relocated to the Mescalero Indian Reservation near Ruidoso, New Mexico, while some remained at Fort Sill. Never again were they allowed to return to their homeland in the Chiricahua Mountains, mainly because of local animosity that remained since the Apache Wars.

It is interesting to note that the Chiricahua Apache were a small force compared to their main adversary, the United States military, which averaged over 5,000 soldiers and 500 Apache Indian scouts in southeastern Arizona. On the national scene after the War Between the States, the postwar army dropped to an average of 26,000 personnel until the advent of the Spanish-American War of 1898. Prior to the Bascom Affair, there were estimates of 1,800 Chiricahua Apache roaming southeastern Arizona. If one includes the Gila Apache of New Mexico, the White Mountain Apache, the Mescalero Apache and other bands that lived in the Sierra Madre of Mexico and elsewhere in the Southwest, that figure would rise to around 8,000. After several decades of numerous skirmishes and deportation by the U.S. Army, along with the ravages of disease and the arrival of Americans with repeating rifles and six-guns, the Chiricahua

Apache population was reduced to several hundred by the turn of the century.

If the decade of the 1880s was the decade of Geronimo, then the 1890s was the decade of the Bronco Apache (sometimes referred to as the Nameless Ones) in southeastern Arizona. These are the Apache who never surrendered to the U.S. military and who escaped to Mexico, settling in the Sierra Madre Mountains. There they established a base of operation with which to attack Mexican settlements, stealing cattle and conducting border raids into Arizona and New Mexico. The Mexican government and local ranchers battled these last Apache into the 1930s. May 1890 brought about increased raids by Bronco Apache into southeastern Arizona. The U.S. military was not as quick to act against the marauding actions of the Bronco Apache. The *Tombstone Epitaph* newspaper went so far as to accuse the U.S. cavalry of cowardice and incompetence when several cowboys were killed and one wounded by Bronco Apache while riding in the neighboring Guadalupe Mountains. However, the Apache were difficult to chase, especially when they separated out in various directions. The Apache could cover between fifty and seventy miles a day, swapping horses along the way while being able to subsist on the fruit of cactus and other plants.

Robert Hardie, a Los Angeles attorney, was ambushed and killed in Rucker Canyon in the Chiricahua Mountains. He was accompanied by his brother-in-law Dr. F. Haynes. Both men were unarmed. After Hardie was shot, Haynes took cover, and discovering his brother-in-law dead, he mounted his horse to escape. A bullet then struck his horse, forcing him to abandon the area by foot. An Apache brave was hot on his trail, firing his rifle into the canyon. Haynes found the horse Hardie had been riding and quickly mounted it, riding to the nearest ranch for help. A group of armed cowboys accompanied Haynes back to the site, where they found Hardie's body mutilated. Scenes like this continued through the 1890s in southeastern Arizona.

Another example of Apache activity in the Chiricahua Mountains occurred on June 12, 1890, a month after the Hardie ambush. While riding in Rucker Canyon, Michael Gray discovered six Apache herding stolen horses from his ranch. Gray took immediate action, opening up on the band of horse thieves at several hundred yards with his Winchester rifle. The Apache fled, leaving the horses behind.

In May 1890, the Bronco Apache threw a scare into the local homesteading population in Bonita Canyon. A male and female Apache robbed a ranch house in Pinery Canyon, killing a homesteader's calf and causing the disappearance of a horse. A moccasin track found in Bonita Canyon alerted Ja Hu Stafford, Neil Erickson and Louis Prue, who, with the aid of troops from neighboring Fort Bowie, unsuccessfully tracked the Bronco Apache. It is reputed that the male Apache was Massai, who escaped from the train that deported many of the Apache to Florida.

Massai, a member of Loco's Chilenne band of Chiricahua Apache, is credited with having raided mining camps and ranches throughout the 1890s into the early 1900s. He was one of several hundred Apache rounded up on a train to Florida in September 1886. Along with several other Apache warriors, including Gray Lizard, he abandoned the prison train in Missouri and journeyed 1,200 miles by foot back to Arizona. Massai and his band were responsible for many raids in the 1890s, including one that involved the murder of Alfred Hands (brother of John and Frank Hands) at his cabin located on the east side of the Chiricahua Mountains near Portal, Arizona, on March 28, 1896.

Public opinion in Arizona territory demanded prompt action by the U.S. military. In April and May 1896, the Seventh Cavalry stationed at Fort Grant, Arizona, sent out a detachment under First Lieutenant Sedgwick Rice to engage the renegade Apache. Leaving the railroad stop at San Simon Station on May 11, 1896, with three Indian scouts and four troopers, the detachment journeyed southward through the Peloncillos until they discovered the trail of the Apache. They also joined up with another detachment of Seventh Cavalry, under the command of Second Lieutenant Nathan King Averill, which was also in pursuit of renegade Apache. The combined force of both detachments included twelve troopers and ten Indian scouts, along with several civilians, including John H. Slaughter, the former sheriff of Cochise County, and his ranch foreman, Jess Fisher.

The last major clash between the U.S. Army and the Apache in Arizona territory occurred on July 17, 1882, at Big Dry Wash, north of Payson. One U.S. cavalryman and sixteen Apache were killed in that battle, followed by the surrender of Geronimo several years later. Skirmishing continued between the U.S military and the Apache for the next fifteen years. On May 17, 1896, Guadalupe Canyon marked the last engagement between the U.S. military and the Apache. It involved the Seventh Cavalry and its raid on a small camp of Apache led by Massai. The location was around a place known as Guadalupe Canyon near the Arizona/New Mexico/Mexico border. Due to a lack of documentation, it remains unclear whether the fight occurred in the American territories or Mexico.

Guadalupe Canyon was considered a strategic pass by the U.S. Army because of its use as an Apache escape route between the United States and

Mexico. It was the famous locality that Lieutenant Charles Gatewood used when escorting Geronimo back into Arizona territory after his surrender in 1886. It was a favorite spot for the U.S. military to guard with soldiers. On the morning of May 16, the Apache camp was spotted by Apache scouts employed by the U.S. military. The camp was located in a pinnacle on a ledge of rock that was practically impregnable, with overhanging rocks making it difficult to surround. The Apache camp consisted of two men and three women. One of the men was presumed to be the elusive Apache Massai. On the morning of May 17, Adelnietze, one of the Apache men who rode with Geronimo a decade earlier, made his presence evident in front of the distant troopers. Several bullets from the troopers felled the Apache warrior, who would later be found by Second Lieutenant Averill's company. The alarm was made, and Massai and the Apache women retreated. Due to the topography and miscommunication on the side of the U.S. Army, they were not apprehended. Although Massai escaped, he would meet his end in September 1906 when he was killed by a group of cowboys near Chloride, New Mexico.

Additional rogue Apache elements in southeastern Arizona included the "Apache Kid," a former Indian scout turned raider and outlaw. He became an Apache scout under the renowned frontiersman Al Seiber. He rose to the rank of first sergeant. However, acts of drunkenness, insubordination and violence in the form of shooting his mentor in the leg led to grievous charges. He was sentenced to ten years' hard labor at the Yuma Territorial Prison in 1889. The Apache Kid, along with several prisoners, escaped en route by overpowering the guards in the stagecoach and killing the sheriff in the ensuing action. A $5,000 reward was offered for his capture. The Apache Kid continued to raid and pillage through the early 1900s. The fate of the Apache Kid remains unknown. Cochise County sheriff John Slaughter claimed to have ambushed and killed the Apache Kid. However, other sources claim that the Apache Kid died of old age in Sonora, Mexico, at an Apache Camp in the early twentieth century.

By the end of the 1890s, Apache raids had decreased as a well-armed settlement became established in southeastern Arizona. However, as late as August 1924, a group of Chiricahua Apache was spotted in the Chiricahua Mountains after having migrated from the Sierra Madre. They killed a cowboy and a horse on their way southeast to the Peloncillo Mountains to gather subsistence in the way of mules. Later, they would return southward through Skeleton Canyon and back down to Mexico through the Animas Valley.

Although few documented hostilities with Apache in Arizona occurred in the 1920s, the opposite was true with regard to Mexico. Apache depredations continued unabated in the Sierra Madre Mountains in northern Mexico. Small bands of marauding Apache roamed an area one hundred miles wide and three hundred miles long consisting of steep-walled canyons, narrow passageways and summits in excess of twelve thousand feet. The State of Sonora, Mexico, hired a force to exterminate the Apache. This private force of gunslingers from both Mexico and the United States was given guns, ammo, food, horses and mules to accomplish the task. Francisco Fimbres, a rancher in northern Sonora, became the leader of this outfit. His wife was killed and son Heraldo Fimbres kidnapped by raiding Apache in Bavispe

Francisco Fimbres, the man for whom the Fimbres expeditions were named, provides three Apache scalps to an anxious audience. Apache maintained their last outpost in the Sierra Madre Mountains of Mexico. *Courtesy* Arizona Daily Star, *March 13, 1931.*

Valley in October 1927. Fimbres vowed to exterminate the Apache presence in northern Sonora. Douglas, Arizona, was the staging ground in the late 1920s and early 1930s that launched what became known as the "Fimbres Apache Expeditions." There was a push among locals to get the Mexican army, along with volunteers from the United States and Canada, involved. Political unrest in Mexico, combined with a distrust of foreign involvement in the confines of Mexico, prevented this from happening. There was also the fear in the Mexican government that such actions would upset its fragile truce with the pacified Yaquis Indians. Ultimately, it was the increase in Mexican settlement in northern Sonora that ended the Apache resistance in the region by the mid-1930s.

Today, the Apache presence can still be felt in the Chiricahua Mountains. While the present-day descendants of the Chiricahua Apache populations are located in Oklahoma and the Mescalero Apache Reservation in southeastern New Mexico, their spiritual presence among the rocks, canyons and trees in their former homeland is unquestionable. Located off U.S. 80, a sixteen-foot-high pyramid commemorates Geronimo's surrender at Skeleton Canyon. It is known among locals as the Geronimo Monument and was dedicated in 1934. The resilience among the Apache is shared by the Chiricahua Mountains themselves, which in 2011 endured the Horseshoe 2 Fire, the worst single fire in modern history of the Chiricahua Mountains.

Chapter 4

Camps and Forts

The U.S. military stationed on the frontier in southeastern Arizona needed several bases of operation from which to operate. The difficulties in managing the Apache Indians in and around the Chiricahua Mountains demanded that temporary military camps and a more permanent fort be built in the confines of that particular region. This was especially the case through the formidable and bloody Apache Pass, often used as an area where Apache waited to ambush unsuspecting military detachments and American settlers traveling west. These forts built in response to this threat included Camp Rucker, located in the southern extent of the Chiricahua Mountains, and Fort Bowie, located in the northern extent of the Chiricahua Mountains.

Camp Rucker, located near the junction of three creeks in White River Canyon (later renamed Rucker Canyon), served as one of the main supply camps in southeastern Arizona between 1878 and 1880. Originally known by the U.S. Army as Camp Supply and briefly as Camp Powers, it was renamed after Lieutenant John Anthony Rucker, who drowned while attempting to rescue fellow officer Lieutenant Austin Henely during a major flooding event in the vicinity on July 11, 1878. Lieutenant Rucker was the son of Daniel Henry Rucker, a major general in the United States Army and brother-in-law to General Phillip Sheridan. He served in the Sixth Cavalry, arriving in Arizona during the summer of 1875. His force was operating in the Mule Mountains in search of Apache. Besides fresh water, Rucker and his command discovered outcroppings of mineralization near the present-day Castle Rock. Rucker had been one of three men—the others included John "Jack" Dunn and T.D. Byrne—to file a mining claim in the Mule Mountains that would later evolve into the renowned billion-dollar mining camp of Bisbee, Arizona.

Throughout its two and a half years of continuous operation, Camp Rucker was manned by the troops of the Sixth Cavalry and Twelfth Infantry, composed of several officers and around 45 enlisted men. Two companies of Indian scouts, commanded by Lieutenants Rucker (Company C) and Austin Henely (Company D), were stationed at the camp, making for a total of 135 men. Camp Rucker was the site of the surrender of Geronimo, Juh and their band of 119 Apache in December 1879. However, Geronimo would later escape, and the site was used again in April 1886 by General Nelson Miles as a temporary supply base for his soldiers in pursuit of Geronimo. After the surrender of Geronimo in September of that year, the camp was abandoned, never to see further military action.

Camp Rucker, sometimes referred to as Fort Rucker, consisted of between ten and fourteen structures, including a hospital, main storehouse, officers' quarters and bakery. The best-preserved buildings on the grounds today are the bakery and the officers' quarters. Many of the other structures were built with logs that had either burned or had been removed. Other buildings with partial walls remaining include the commissary and the medical supply cabin. A post Traders Store once existed close to the medical supply cabin. No remains of it are readily seen today.

The site later became a ranching headquarters for the twenty-two-thousand-acre Old Camp Rucker Ranch of cattleman Michael Gray, who also served as justice of the peace in Tombstone. Gray sold the ranch in 1896, and it passed to several owners, including Theodore and Mathilde Hampe and Charles and Mary Rak. Although not part of the original camp, the ranch house remains, having been built in 1930. The land was acquired by Mrs. Ella Dana in 1943 and used as a retreat until the property was transferred to the U.S. Forest Service in 1970. A manmade three-and-a-half-acre lake nearby was named after Lieutenant Rucker. Rucker Canyon Lake was regularly stocked by the Arizona Game and Fish Department with trout. The lake was the victim of a landslide in 1992 caused by heavy rains that occurred after the Rattlesnake Fire. Lack of vegetation caused soil displacement and the filling in of the former lake with sediment caused by debris flow. All that remains at present of the lake site is a grassy meadow. The remains of Camp Rucker are accessible by traveling 22.0 miles east on West Rucker Canyon Road from Highway 191 South. This washboard

The wooden barn and stables seen here at Camp Rucker played an indirect role in the history of Tombstone. In July 1880, several mules were stolen from the locality by the McLaury brothers of Tombstone. The U.S. military called on U.S. Deputy Marshal Virgil Earp to track down the party involved in the apprehension of the mules, which were discovered with altered brands on the McLaury brothers' ranch. *Courtesy of Lorie Cavalli.*

Although there is documentation that officers' quarters as well as the enlisted men's quarters were stockade tents composed of vertical log walls and canvas roofs, there is a possibility that this adobe structure was built in 1880 to accommodate the officers stationed at the camp. This is a view of the officers' quarters as it appears in 2013. *Courtesy of William Ascarza.*

Included in this photo are Charles Rak, cattleman of the Old Camp Rucker Ranch, and W.H. Hughes discussing a Civilian Conservation Corps project around 1937 at Rucker Canyon. *Courtesy of United States Department of Agriculture.*

dirt back road is accommodating to passenger vehicles. Proceed on Rucker Canyon Road 0.7 miles past the Camp Rucker Group Use Area turnoff. A field with a chain-link fence is seen on the left-hand side of the road. If you park in front of the fence, enter through the gate and walk several hundred feet along the trail, Old Fort Rucker lies just beyond the streambed.

Located on the eastern entrance to Apache Pass, Fort Bowie operated from July 28, 1862, until its closure on October 17, 1894. Named for General George W. Bowie of the California Volunteers, Fort Bowie was created by General James Carleton after the Battle of Apache Pass to establish a line of communication with his forces and California and also as a response to the open warfare between the Apache chief Cochise and the United States military. Nearby Apache Spring was the only reliable source of water for many miles. The availability of water made Apache Pass the preferred travel route for migrants and a strategic locality on which to build a fort.

American history of Apache Pass dates back to 1854, when a survey party was sent to the area following the Gadsden Purchase to access the potential of using the land as a future route for the Southern Pacific Railroad. Lieutenant John G. Parke, a topographic engineer in the U.S. Army, is credited with having mapped a route through Apache Pass. In 1858, John Butterfield established a station for the Overland Mail near the future site of Fort Bowie. Operating between the years of 1858 and the beginning of the War Between the States in 1861, the Butterfield Company ran its stagecoaches through the pass, which was also a prime spot for ambushes carried out by the Chiricahua Apache.

The Battle of Apache Pass occurred in July 1862 between part of General Carleton's command and the Apache led by Mangas Coloradas and Cochise as Carleton's California Volunteers reclaimed territory in both present-day Arizona and New Mexico that was formerly occupied by the Confederacy. The Battle of Apache Pass would be the first time the United States used field artillery against the Apache. Conflict between the Apache and the U.S. army, ignited by the Bascom Affair the previous year, would continue for the next thirty-five years.

During its existence, Fort Bowie provided the U.S. Army with a command center to protect settlements in southeastern Arizona from raids carried out by the Chiricahua Apache. Pinery Canyon was the location that supplied pine timbers for the buildings at Fort Bowie. Chief Cochise visited the post trader building at Fort Bowie on several occasions during the peace of the 1870s to socialize with the U.S. military. It was the military members stationed at Fort Bowie who pursued the raids of Geronimo and Natchez. When Geronimo finally surrendered, he and his followers were brought to Fort Bowie as prisoners of war en route to their confinement in Florida. Fort Bowie remained in operation eight years after Geronimo surrendered, although the Apache threat had greatly dissipated. After Fort Bowie was decommissioned on October 17, 1894, it was abandoned, and its buildings and its 2,400 acres were later sold in a public action in Phoenix on June 20, 1911. Created by an act of Congress on August 30, 1964, Fort Bowie is classified as a National Historic Site that today encompasses 1,000 acres. The remains of the fort are accessible to the public by taking Highway 186 south twenty miles from Willcox and then heading eight miles east on unpaved Apache Pass Road to the parking lot and trailhead. From the trailhead, it is approximately a three-mile round trip to the remains of the fort and back.

The town of Bowie is located off Interstate 10, twenty-five miles east of Willcox and fifteen miles north of the remains of Fort Bowie. Originally named Teviston after Captain James Tevis, a filibuster who partook in William Walker's campaign to acquire Nicaragua for the United States in 1856, the town was established in 1880. He also served as an agent for the Butterfield Overland Stage Line at Apache Pass and as a Confederate army officer during the War Between the States. After the war, he settled in Texas, returning to Arizona fifteen years later to open a store and to

This distant view is of the officers' quarters and barracks as they existed at Fort Bowie just prior to its closing in 1894. *Courtesy of Fort Bowie National Historic Site.*

The remains of Fort Bowie as they exist today preserved at the Fort Bowie National Historic Site. *Courtesy of William Ascarza.*

work on a series of mining claims in the Dos Cabezas Mountains under the Cochise Mining and Milling Company. The Southern Pacific Railroad crossed near his property, and a town was established, originally known as Teviston. However, that name was later changed to Bowie on account of a local railroad stationmaster named Bean who wanted the town to bear his name. Tevis cautioned Bean against naming the town after him since the town's residents subsisted on a daily diet of beans, and they had already had a bellyful. The feud continued between Tevis and Bean, with Bean giving up using his name and eventually calling the town Bowie Station. Conflict between Tevis and Bean over the town's name resulted in Bean successfully using his influence to change the town's name to Bowie by 1911, several years after Tevis passed away.

The heliograph was used frequently during the Indian Wars in southeastern Arizona. The heliograph optimized the use of light as a means of transmission. The bending of light using multiple mirrors to transmit Morse code was an important tool for the U.S. Army in the field. These transmissions were used to coordinate the U.S. military's movement and reveal the Apache location among the vast valleys and mountain ranges in southeastern Arizona. The heliograph station above Fort Bowie at Bowie Peak is said to have relayed over 334 messages during the final Apache campaign by the U.S. military against Geronimo.

Temporary camps were sometimes built with the intent of versatility in tracking their Apache opponent and for heliograph usage. Named after Colonel Sterling Price, who served in the Mexican War, Camp Price was located southeast of Camp Rucker in the southern end of the Chiricahua Mountains. Camp Price served as a military outpost in the early 1880s, and a military telegraph station was located at the site.

Another temporary camp was named after a U.S. Army captain who lost his life pursuing renegade Apache. Camp Emmet Crawford was established near Galeyville in 1886, near the junction of Onion Creek and Turkey Creek, a place known as Soldier Flat at the base of Silver Peak. It served the purpose of protecting citizens from groups of marauding Apache after the surrender of Geronimo. However, it was ephemeral, lasting only several months since Geronimo surrendered that same year.

Chapter 5

Pioneers

One of the most successful means by which the United States settled the western frontier was the passage of the Homestead Act in 1862. Its purpose was the distribution of land to the American people in exchange for its care and cultivation. The stipulations for application of a homestead included the following: The individual had to be twenty-one years of age and reside on the specified land, consisting of 160 acres, within six months of filing the claim. He also had to reside on the land for the next five years, cultivating it when necessary. Several amendments to the original Homestead Act of 1862 made it more attractive for individuals to homestead land, such as reducing the residency requirements and increasing the land allotment. After the removal of the Chiricahua Indian Reservation in 1876, land in the Chiricahua Mountains opened up to homesteading, which peaked in the region during the early twentieth century. The increase in homesteading in the Chirichua Mountains served several purposes, including providing cheap land and building material, access to the abundant grasses in Sulphur Spring Valley and nearby natural springs and protection by the local army contingent located at Fort Bowie. Some of the more renowned pioneers in the Chiricahua Mountains included Stephen Reed, Ja Hu Stafford, the Erickson family, the Riggs family and John Hands.

The earliest homesteading in the Chiricahua Mountains occurred at Cave Creek Canyon, located on the eastside of the Chiricahua Mountains. Cave Creek Cienega/Cienega Spring was known as a reliable source of water. Cave Creek Canyon has been referred to as the Yosemite of the

The smooth monolith of Cathedral Rock, in excess of seven hundred feet in height, is a landmark in Cave Creek Canyon. Traveling west from its prominence leads to the center of the Chiricahua Mountains. *Courtesy of William Ascarza.*

West. Homesteaders were attracted to the abundant vegetation and animal species fed by the waters of Cave Creek. They were also attracted to the geologic diversity in the area, including the impressive Cathedral Rock, which attains a height of over 6,800 feet. The mixture of cottonwood and sycamore trees in the vicinity of North Fork and Cave Creek made this area the choice locale in which to establish the American Museum of Natural History's Southwestern Research Station, the early focus of which was to study invertebrates found in the Chiricahua Mountains.

The property on which the Southwestern Research Station currently sits was originally occupied by Stephen B. Reed. Stephen Reed, a Missourian and pioneer, was one of the original homesteaders in the Chiricahua Mountains. During the California Gold Rush, Reed stopped briefly in Arizona on his way to prospect for gold in California, only to return twenty years later in 1879. That same year, Reed built a log cabin using native alligator juniper and ponderosa pine. Stephen Reed built the first wagon road into the canyon at Cave Creek. According to many sources, the Reed family was the first non-native family to settle in the Chiricahua Mountains. Reed formed Painted Canyon Ranch, a settlement that he would inhabit until his death in 1912. During that time, Reed sold vegetables to Galeyville and traded with Silver City, New Mexico. By 1910, the water from Cave Creek provided Reed, along with local farmers, an opportunity to harvest water for their crops through irrigation. Reed courted the acceptance of all local inhabitants, including the Chiricahua Apache and the outlaws at Galeyville. The Reed Cabin remains intact near the main office of the Southwestern Research Station. It functions as a private residence and may be the oldest intact homestead in southeastern Arizona.

The property was sold to John Hands in 1915. Hands had worked for Stephen Reed since 1887, having emigrated with his family from England. Both John Hands and his brother Frank had homesteads in the North Fork of Pinery Canyon near Horsefall Canyon. Hands, an entrepreneur, sought to establish vacation rentals on the property, changing the name to the "Bide-a-wee Ranch" in 1919. Several years later, the ranch was sold to Frank W. Officer, who planned to establish both a resort and a dude ranch on the property. Financial troubles hindered the expansion of the ranch, and it was sold to Harry A. and Emma M. Clark in 1926. The Clarks made improvements to the ranch in the form of completing the construction of the main house and the erection of a springhouse and a spring-fed concrete swimming pool, with a constant water temperature of seventy-two degrees.

The man at far right, possibly John Hands, was involved with the Rock Circle Trail Camp on the Chiricahua Division in 1924. *Courtesy of United States Department of Agriculture.*

The Southwestern Research Station (SWRS) located in Cave Creek was the site of the original homestead of Stephen Reed in 1879. Reed was from Missouri and is known for having built the first wagon road in Cave Creek. Since 1955, the year-round field station has been under the guidance of the American Museum of Natural History and serves as a base of operations for scientific studies in the Chiricahua Mountains. *Courtesy of William Ascarza.*

The ranch went through multiple ownerships over the next thirty years, with the plumbing and wiring of the main house and the establishment of several guest quarters. By 1953, the ranch had come to the attention of Dr. Mont Cazier, the chairman of the Department of Insects and Spiders at the American Museum of Natural History in New York. Cazier wanted to acquire the site to serve as a biological field station for his institute. Owners Weldon F. and Phyllis W. Heald were both freelance writers and frowned on the initial idea of selling. Weldon F. Heald served as the director of the Sierra Club from 1945 through 1949. However, by 1955, they had a financial change of heart and sold their ranch to the American Museum of Natural History in New York. The funding for the purchase was provided by David Rockefeller, who gave $53,000 for the land and all of its furnishings. The Southwest Research Station was established that year, with Dr. Mont Cazier serving as its first director.

Over the next several decades, the Southwest Research Station continued to grow with additional funding and support from Dr. David Rockefeller, Dr. Albert E. Parr and others, including local landowners who donated acreage. By the 1990s and 2000s, through funding of the National Science Foundation and American Museum of Natural History, additional laboratories and dormitories and a wastewater treatment system had been built to accommodate the needs of the visiting researchers. As of 2010, the Southwest Research Station partnered with the U.S. Fish and Wildlife and Arizona Game and Fish Departments to reintroduce endangered species back into the Chiricahua Mountains, including the Chiricahua leopard frog.

Located on the banks of Cave Creek is the Herb Martyr Campground. A nearby dam by the same name was built in 1935 and christened after Herb Martyr, a worker who was killed during its construction. The area affords many scenic attractions, with elevation averages of 5,800 feet and camping amenities surrounded by oak trees, including tent sites, grills and picnic tables. Fred Winn served as forest supervisor in the area during the entire operation of the Civilian Conservation Corps. Winn had a 365-foot waterfall named after him known today as Winn Falls. During winter, the waterfall freezes, appearing as a massive cluster of icicles.

Another early homestead in the Chiricahua Mountains was owned by Ja Hu Stafford. Stafford, a North Carolinian, migrated across the country from Illinois, Wyoming and Montana before finally settling in Arizona Territory to escape the harsh winters in the northern states. Stafford married Pauline Amelia Madsen, a Mormon whose family he wintered with while traveling to Arizona. Stafford selected Bonita Canyon in the Chiricahua Mountains to homestead. Prior to his wife's death in 1893 at the age of twenty-six, the couple had seven children, four of whom lived to adulthood.

The Stafford Cabin remains standing today and is one of the earliest surviving log cabins in southeastern Arizona. The cabin is one of the major attractions in the confines of Chiricahua National Monument. The original cabin contained two rooms that measured thirteen by twelve feet. These rooms were probably built in the early 1880s, shortly after Stafford filed his application to homestead 160 acres in October 1880.

Stafford was a renowned gardener and architect. He had several vegetable gardens, along with orchards of apple, pear and peach trees. He devised an irrigation system that drew water from nearby springs east of Bonita Canyon. His gardens and orchards supplied local neighbors and the soldiers at Fort Bowie, until the latter was decommissioned in 1894. Some of the vegetables included cabbage, lettuce and turnips. The upper garden of Stafford's cabin later served as the site of a CCC camp in the 1930s. The logs he used to build his cabin were hand-hewn from juniper and pine bark beetle-killed trees. These trees were selected because of their abundant

The Stafford cabin is depicted here in 1910, with Ja Hu Stafford and his youngest daughter on the west side of the building. The cabin was later purchased by the Erickson daughters to further expand their Faraway guest ranch facilities. The cabin remains in existence today, located 450 yards from the Faraway Ranch House, and is one of the oldest log structures in Arizona. It was placed on the National Register of Historic Places on March 31, 1975. *Courtesy of Library of Congress Prints and Photographs Division.*

pitch, which acted as a sealant protecting them from deterioration due to the elements of nature. Stafford fashioned his windowsills from alligator juniper because of its resistance to moisture. Other homesteaders did not fare as well as Stafford. One such settler was Frank Pack, a miner who built a home and orchard near Ash Spring in the 1940s. Within a decade, his home was burned to the ground by a lightning-induced fire.

Stafford's daughter Clara S. Wheeler inherited the homestead after his death in 1913. She, in turn, sold the cabin and 160 acres to Lillian and Hildegarde Erickson five years later. The Ericksons used this land and cabin to enhance their dude ranch. Faraway Ranch owed its humble beginning to the adventurous and persevering spirit of Swedish emigrants Neil and Emma Erickson, who met at Fort Bowie. Neil Erickson's father had immigrated to the United States from Sweden several decades prior to Neil and was killed by Indians while working on the Northern Pacific Railroad. Upon arriving in the United States in 1879, one of Neil's first inclinations was to join the military and fight Indians as a means of retribution for the fate that befell his father. First Sergeant Neil Erickson was a soldier in the U.S. Army while Emma Peterson was a family servant for an officer at Fort Bowie. Neil Erickson would serve five years with the U.S. cavalry. After the surrender of Geronimo, Emma Peterson purchased a property in Bonita Canyon that would later become the nucleus of the Faraway Guest Ranch. Both Neil and Emma were married at the Cosmopolitan Hotel in Tucson in 1887 and afterward relocated to several localities during the course of a year that involved hospitality ventures operating boardinghouses for miners and railroad men. In July 1888, they finally settled on the property that Emma Erickson had acquired earlier in Bonita Canyon. Their children included Hildegarde, Lillian and Ben Erickson. Neil Erickson worked a number of jobs, including as a mechanic, miner and carpenter, and he built and lived on several properties in Bisbee in order to make money. In 1903, he was appointed a ranger for the U.S. Forest Service.

The Riggses, a prominent ranching family, homesteaded on land three miles west of the Erickson Ranch. Brannick Riggs was a native of Alabama and a Confederate veteran who was wounded at the Battle of Shiloh/Pittsburg Landing. Riggs and his wife sought their fortunes in California after the war. Along the way, they settled in Sulphur Spring Valley at an area that later became known in the 1880s as the Riggs Settlement. The Riggs family became cattle ranchers, selling beef to Fort Bowie. They also provided lumber to the growing homestead population. Brannick Riggs built a sawmill near Pinery Canyon in the 1890s. Ja Hu Stafford acquired the lumber for his homestead from the Riggs sawmill. By 1904, the Riggs Cattle Company was formed and later dissolved in 1922. The Riggs family was extensive, with eleven children. The Riggses even hosted a local post office in the area known as Brannick or Brannock, operating from August 16, 1887, to April 1, 1891. By 1929, the Riggs family holdings included 100,000 acres of patented land, along with 50,000 acres of leased property and 25,000 acres of forest lands.

In 1917, Hildegarde and later her sister Lillian Erickson opened their ranch up to visitors, making it a dude ranch. They would acquire Ja Hu Stafford's property and add it to their guest ranch the following year. They offered their guests horseback riding into the rhyolite pinnacles and Bonita Canyon. Lillian Erickson, who later married Ed Riggs, grandson of Brannick Riggs, named the ranch "Faraway" because it was so far away from everything. The nearest towns were at a minimum of forty miles away through undeveloped country on dirt roads. Faraway Ranch was a working ranch that included over five hundred head of cattle. The ranch included the perennial waters of Bonita Creek lined on either side with oak trees.

Faraway Ranch served as the gateway to the "Wonderland of Rocks" in the Chiricahua Mountains, as it became known through advertisement by Lillian and Ed Riggs. They built trails and led tours on horseback through the "Wonderland of Rocks." Lillian and Ed Riggs advertised the beauty of the area with their photos of rock formations at local fairs, civic group meetings and in correspondence with Washington, D.C. Their perseverance in advertising the surrounding beauty of the area was rewarded by President Calvin Coolidge on April 18, 1924, with the establishment of Chiricahua National Monument. The purpose was to protect the unique rock pinnacles. With the influx of tourist visitation to the monument, the Riggses were able to capitalize on their dude ranch since it was the only lodging and restaurant in the area. They also were able to increase their cattle-ranching venture. Ten years later, other factors increased visitation to the ranch, including the building of a road into the National Monument and the public works of the Civilian Conservation Corps. Part of the Riggses' property was leased by the federal government for the establishment of a CCC camp. Ed Riggs hired on as the trail foreman, providing additional money to help sustain the eight-thousand-acre Faraway Guest Ranch during the years of the Great Depression.

Calvin Coolidge is credited with having created Chiricahua National Monument on April 18, 1924. The legislation stated from Presidential Proclamation No. 1692 (43 Stat. 1946): "Whereas, certain natural formations, known as 'The Pinnacles,' with the Coronado National Forest, in the State of Arizona, are of scientific interest, and it appears that the public interests will be promoted by reserving as much land as may be necessary for the proper protection thereof, as a National Monument." *Courtesy of Library of Congress Prints and Photographs Division.*

Acquired by the National Park Service in June 1979, both Faraway Ranch and Stafford Cabin remain preserved and are classified as living history museums. They are open year round for tours upon request through the National Park Service employees. At the entrance

Above: A spectacular view is seen from the balanced rock formation across the Wonderland of Rocks looking west toward the Sulphur Springs Valley and the Dos Cabezas Mountains. *Courtesy of National Park Service Harpers Ferry Center Collections.*

Left: Lillian and Ed Riggs, along with guest Anna Marie Powers and a friendly dog, pose for the camera at the Faraway Ranch House in 1938. *Courtesy of Library of Congress Prints and Photographs Division.*

This image depicts men on horseback at Faraway Ranch during the 1920s, when it operated as a dude ranch. *Courtesy of Library of Congress Prints and Photographs Division.*

to Chiricahua National Monument is the Ericksons' cemetery, including the final resting places of Neil, Emma, Ben and Hildegard Erickson. Lillian is buried several miles away at the Riggs family cemetery. Near the Erickson grave site is the grave of Louis Prue, who was one of the earliest settlers in Bonita Canyon. He received a patent on his 160-acre homestead in 1891. Louis Prue, a Chiricahua rancher and former U.S. Army scout under General George Crook, wanted to be buried at the mouth of Bonita Canyon so that he could view his cattle pass by on their way to get water from the nearby Bonita and Pinery Canyon Creeks. He met a premature death from falling off a horse.

Perhaps one of the most distinct individuals who lived in the Chiricahua Mountains was John Hands. John Hands, along with his brothers Frank and Alfred, emigrated to the United States from England. Alfred Hands was killed by Apache in the Chiricahua Mountains in 1895. Some sources claim that he was the last person killed by an Apache in Arizona. Some of John Hands's diverse interests included mining, ranching and archaeology. He was known to have collected many antiquities of early Americana in the Southwest. His notable excavations of Indian irrigation projects around Cave Creek included some dating back several thousand years. John and Frank Hands were responsible for building the road from Pinery Canyon to Portal. Because of this feat, the pass in Pinery Canyon became known as Hands Pass.

Headstones of some of the original pioneers in the Chiricahua Mountains still exist. In addition to Alfred Hands, Mary Bridger's grave is also found in the Chiricahua Mountains in Bonita Park, south of the King of Lead Mine Road. Mary Bridger was part of a pioneer family who lived out of a cabin at the turn of the century. Mary's husband, Tom, was a prospector in the Chiricahua Mountains. Mary passed away in 1902, and her grave was marked with a marble headstone by the Riggs family. Although the cabin no longer exists, traces of an old wagon road connecting Whitetail Pass to Bonita Park remain to this day. Another headstone represents the demise of another Chiricahua Mountain inhabitant, Frank C. Caldwell, who was murdered by one-armed Jim Gould in a dispute over a woman. He was shot in the back while leaving his mining prospect in Jhus Canyon on July 26, 1903. Although Jim Gould claimed self-defense, he was sent to Yuma Territorial Prison. His early release was due to the closure of the prison in 1909. Jim later resided in the San Simon Valley.

Chapter 6

Lost Treasure

Tales of hidden treasure abound in the American West, especially during the latter half of the nineteenth century, when train robberies were rife. Because of the remoteness of the Chiricahua Mountains, they were a natural destination for some of southeastern Arizona's most notorious outlaws, including Black Jack Ketchum, Curly Bill Brocius, Johnny Ringo and the Clanton Gang. Leslie Canyon was named for the notorious outlaw Buckskin Frank Leslie, who owned the 7-Up Ranch in Horseshoe Valley. Leslie had many occupations, including bartender, cattleman, gambler and murderer. Legend has it that he used the dance hall girl he was living with for target practice, tracing her outline on the wall of their ranch house. He was sent to Yuma Territorial Prison for killing this girl on the ranch in 1889. Some sources claim that it was Buckskin Frank Leslie who killed the outlaw Johnny Ringo at West Turkey Creek in the Chiricahua Mountains.

Other than cattle rustling and occasional civil disturbances in the Chiricahua Mountains perpetrated by the outlaws, there are also tales of hidden treasure in the range. Some of the most well known in and around the Chiricahua Mountains include the tale of outlaws Zwing Hunt and Billy Grounds, who hid $3 million in gold and silver in a remote location on the eastern foothills of the Chiricahua Mountains near Harris Mountain, six miles northwest of the town of Portal. Curly Bill Brocius and Johnny Ringo were heavily involved in cattle rustling and robberies in southeastern Arizona. It is said that Curly Bill had a following of anywhere from forty to one hundred men, whom he would use to carry out his criminal activities.

One of his favorite operations involved intercepting Mexican bandits who smuggled their stolen goods to localities in southern Arizona, including Tucson. Legend has it that some of his men overtook a group of Mexican smugglers in July 1881 at a mass of jumbled rocks known as Devil's Kitchen in Skeleton Canyon in the Peloncillo Mountains. They caught the Mexicans by surprise, killing every last one of them and acquiring $75,000. After dividing up their proceeds, they returned to their base of operations in Galeyville, spending most of it supporting the local economy at the bars and poker tables over the course of a month.

Soon after, another robbery—this one greatly exceeding the former—took place again at Devil's Kitchen. Jim Hughes, an associate of Curly Bill's operating down in Mexico as an agent provocateur, heard of a party of Mexican smugglers moving $300,000 in gold and silver bars via mule train through the same route as the earlier hijacked expedition. Brocius was away at the time of the robberies and unaware of Jim Hughes's plans. Hughes figured he would handle the job himself and convinced Zwing Hunt, a muleskinner, along with young outlaw Billy Grounds and five local Galeyville inhabitants, to take part in the robbery. They arrived in Skeleton Canyon, the site of the previous ambush. They took the Mexican pack train, which consisted of fifteen men and thirty mules, by surprise that morning, killing six Mexicans and leaving nine of the smugglers fleeing for their lives.

Upon routing their quarry, both Zwing Hunt and Billy Grounds found that they lacked the pack animals and wagons to move the treasure. They decided that it was best to bury the treasure in a nearby canyon until they found a better means to extradite it. Jim Hughes never revealed to Curly Bill his involvement regarding the raid. However, Hughes's fortunes soured when he entrusted Grounds and Hunt to stash the loot. Days after completing the task, the two were gunned down in a fight with other outlaws. Hunt survived, though he ultimately succumbed to death because of his wound. He revealed on his deathbed in San Antonio, Texas, that he and Grounds hid the loot at the foot of Davis Mountain somewhere between Willcox and Lordsburg. Local sources, including Bill Sanders, who operated a ranch on West Turkey Creek, believe the site to be present-day Harris Mountain in the Chiricahua Mountains. Although Sanders never reported finding the treasure, Sanders Peak was named after him.

Another example of hidden treasure in the Chiricahua Mountains involved Black Jack Ketchum, who stashed several thousand dollars acquired from his robberies, including one at a bank in Nogales in 1884 and another involving a Southern Pacific Railroad holdup. It is believed that the cache from these robberies was hidden in a cave known as "Room Forty Four" in Wild Cat Canyon at the south end of the Chiricahua Mountains, eight miles southwest of Portal. However, no conclusive evidence has ever been reported about its discovery. Some speculation that the value of treasure stashed at Wild Cat Canyon was fabricated came from the gang's reputation of spending their profits of theft quickly and carelessly. They were not known for having the patience of hiding their profits from their robberies for any amount of time.

Treasure hunters have surveyed the Chiricahua Mountains for years in search of hidden outlaw caches. One such hunter who had a sizable collection of historic artifacts was Orville Mickens (March 12, 1920–August 11, 2007). He opened Frontier Relics Museum to the general public in 1981. The museum was located right off State Highway 186 in Dos Cabezas, fourteen miles south of Willcox. Orville's museum consisted of artifacts that he collected across southeast Arizona from 1940 up until the early 2000s. His vast collection of items included opium bottles, barbed wire, cast-iron toys, blacksmith tools, saloon tokens, rifles, pistols and a variety of military collectibles dating back to the Apache Wars. Some of his most exceptional finds included a loaded rocket from the era of Pancho Villa, a brass Spanish conquistador's stirrup from 1540 and a 1950 Cadillac in the back of the barn that he offered for sale at $15,000.

Orville Mickens collected and displayed history in Cochise County and knew every back road and off-road locality in and around the Chiricahua Mountains. *Courtesy of William Ascarza.*

Orville Mickens hailed from Roberts, Illinois. He worked as a vehicle mechanic for the Sulphur Springs Valley Electric Cooperative, Inc., until retiring in 1982. His hobby was collecting and displaying history for others to see and learn from. He

The public hanging of Black Jack Ketchum on October 5, 1900, in Clayton, New Mexico, drew a crowd. *Courtesy of Western Americana Postcards.*

enjoyed War Between the States history and Indian Wars history. He visited ghost towns, caves and forts. His regular job was exciting at times, too. He was once asked to travel on a pack mule to the top of a mountain in Texas Canyon to service diesel equipment. His real passion was the history of Cochise County, with emphasis on the Indian Wars and pioneer settlement along with mining history. His giveaway table consisted of glass bottles, mining crucibles and minerals that he collected over the years. One of Orville's favorite stomping grounds was the Chiricahua Mountains, which he frequented.

Chapter 7

Chiricahua National Monument and the Surrounding Chiricahua Wilderness

Chiricahua National Monument and the surrounding Chiricahua Wilderness are two of the great attractions in southeastern Arizona. Today the Chiricahua Mountains are part of Coronado National Forest, a noncontiguous national forest in southeastern Arizona. Coronado National Forest consists of five districts, including Sierra Vista, Nogales, Safford, Santa Catalina and Douglas, which together encompass two million acres of land. The Chiricahua Mountains are under the supervision of the Douglas Ranger Station.

The difference between a national park and a national monument is the type of legislation that establishes its existence. A park is created by an act of Congress, in contrast to a monument, historic site or battlefield, which are designated as national monuments by presidential signature. National monuments receive less funding than national parks and are more commonly found in the American Southwest. The purpose for the National Park Service, which manages both national parks and monuments, is to establish recreational sites for the American people, while the purpose of the U.S. Forest Service is to manage the natural resources. National forests are open to logging, mining, grazing and hunting, in contrast to the status of a national park or monument, where everything is protected. The Chiricahua Wilderness, located south of the Chiricahua National Monument and managed by the U.S. Forest Service, encompasses an area of twenty-eight square miles in the central part of the Chiricahua Mountains, which includes the high points of the mountain range, including Chiricahua Peak.

Because of the great westward migration of settlement during the latter quarter of the nineteenth century, the United States government began to address the need for natural resource conservation. One of the first steps occurred in 1891 when Congress passed the General Land Law Revision Act. This enabled the president to set aside portions of public land as timber reserves to be managed by the Department of the Interior. Initially called "forest reserves," they were the predecessors of what became in 1907 "national forests" that were transferred to the jurisdiction of the Department of Agriculture. The national forest caused a decline in abusive logging practices in the Chiricahua Mountains. Coronado National Forest, established in 1908, was the product of three forest reserves, including the Santa Rita, Santa Catalina and Dragoon. In 1917, the U.S. Forest Service operation in the Chiricahua Mountains was reorganized with the addition of the Chiricahua National Forest with the district as part of the Coronado Forest.

The origin of land preservation in the Chiricahua Mountains began in the early twentieth century. During the administration of President Theodore Roosevelt, there was an ardent push to protect land in the American West from development while conserving natural resources. The Chiricahua Forest Reserve was created in 1902 as a response to the need for protecting the land from overgrazing of cattle and development because of excessive homesteading. It also served to protect the timber and water resources of the Chiricahua Mountains. The Chiricahua Forest Reserve was managed by the Department of the Interior's General Land Office and later the Department of Agriculture. Forest Ranger Charles T. McGlone was appointed to oversee the operations in early 1903. He was to supervise two employees, who included ex-sergeant Neil Erickson and Ed Riggs. The tasks at hand included managing rangeland among the local ranchers and operating fire patrols from the vantage point of a two-room building used as a fire lookout near Barfoot Park during the summer monsoon. The average monthly pay for the rangers was sixty dollars. Their out-of-pocket expenses were transportation, which included their own saddle horse, and accouterments such as a compass, shovel and axe.

Neil Erickson was responsible for resource management in the Chiricahua Mountains during his employment with the U.S. Forest Service. Erickson built a ranger station on Soldier Flat, which was the site of the former U.S. Army Camp Crawford. He also supervised the construction of a fire lookout tower on Chiricahua Peak in 1912. Ed Riggs coined the name Massai Point for the high point in the national monument after the Chiricahua Apache Massai, whom his future father-in-law, Neil Erickson, had tracked in the Wonderland of Rocks back in the 1890s. Massai had been accused of stealing a horse from the U.S. military.

When Chiricahua National Monument was established by presidential proclamation on April 18, 1924, to preserve and protect its natural rock formations, it was administered by the U.S. Forest Service. It was not until 1933 that the National Park Service acquired jurisdiction over Chiricahua National Monument. It was during this period that the Coronado National Forest began to develop Chiricahua National Monument so as to improve accessibility for the surrounding community. As a result, an eight-mile stretch of road known as Bonita Canyon Highway was developed in September 1934 by the Civilian Conservation Corps to further provide access to the monument.

Today, Chiricahua National Monument has 11,985 acres, of which 10,290 acres are designated wilderness. Most of the land north, east and south of Chiricahua National Monument is managed by the U.S. Department of Agriculture and Forest Service. The land south and southeast of the monument includes the 87,700-acre Chiricahua Wilderness. The Chiricahua Wilderness can be accessed through Turkey Creek, Rucker Canyon, Rustler Park and Cave Creek. In recent years, Chiricahua National Monument averaged sixty thousand visitors a year. Chiricahua National Monument is open year round. Camping amenities in Bonita Canyon Campground consists of twenty-four individual campsites for RVs and tents.

Camping in Bonita Canyon Campground can be an enlivening experience. This is especially the case when the nearby creek is running with water during the monsoon season. Additional campgrounds in the Chiricahua Mountains include the Pinery Canyon Campground, Rustler Park Campground, Idlewilde Campground and Sunny Flat Campground. *Courtesy of William Ascarza.*

Despite the relative ease and tranquility that goes with the job of being a park ranger in a remote region of land, the challenges facing park rangers have become greater in recent decades. Conflicts with illegal aliens, drug runners, poachers and the natural elements themselves are cause for major concern. In recent years, several park rangers have been killed in the line of duty. Seasonal law enforcement ranger Randy Morgenson, who died from hypothermia after falling through a snowdrift at Sequoia and Kings Canyon National Parks, is one such example. His remains were discovered in 2001, five years after his disappearance. Another such incident involved ranger Jeff Christensen, who perished after falling from a mountain trail in Rocky Mountain National Park, Colorado. A third instance involved park ranger Kris Eggle, who was killed in the line of duty in 2002 at Organ Pipe Cactus National Monument while pursuing drug runners from Mexico who had crossed the border. Organ Pipe Cactus National Monument has gained the notorious reputation of one of the most dangerous parks in the nation.

In the Chiricahua Mountains, one of the most curious and unsolved cases involved the disappearance of law enforcement ranger Paul Fugate on the afternoon of January 13, 1980. Fugate left the visitor center to check the nature trail on foot to Faraway Ranch and never returned. Paul Fugate was the only modern National Park Service employee whose disappearance remains a mystery. His body has yet to be discovered. His disappearance brought a plethora of media attention to Chiricahua National Monument. Possible explanations for his disappearance included drug smuggling, illegal immigration, confrontation with poachers and trappers, marriage problems or simply walking away from his job and life. Prior to his disappearance, Fugate had evicted trappers out of the park, and their equipment may have been confiscated by Fugate. One report had a man who looked like Fugate being seen in a pickup truck heading north toward Willcox, perhaps with trappers. However, none of these explanations has proven substantial. Southern Arizona Search and Rescue conducted an exhaustive search, yet no remains have been found to this writing in 2013.

Chapter 8

Civilian Conservation Corps

The Civilian Conservation Corps was an important contributor to the maintenance of the natural resources of the Chiricahua Mountains. The purpose of the Civilian Conservation Corps was the conservation of natural resources through the employment of young men who were directly in need of work due to the effects of the Great Depression. They became known as the "Tree Army." Established by President Franklin Roosevelt, the Civilian Conservation Corps operated during the years of 1933 through 1942, with 2.5 million young men on its roster during its years of operation. The Civilian Conservation Corps became informally known as the CCC in 1937. In the early days, the CCC was almost twice the size of the U.S. Army, consisting of 500,000 men. Enrollees were organized into companies, and the companies were assigned to camps. Camps were designed to contain 200 enrollees.

The Civilian Conservation Corps provided work for single young men between the ages of eighteen and twenty-five in all forty-eight states, Alaska Territory, Hawaii Territory, Puerto Rico and the Virgin Islands. There were 118 CCC camps in National Park Service areas across the county. Enrollees earned thirty dollars a month, twenty-five of which was sent back to support their dependents, and their involvement in the CCC was limited to one or two years. The CCC completed works projects including tree planting, dam building, road and bridge construction, firefighting and suppression and telephone and power line installation. Its motto was, "We can take it!" Today's fire suppression crews are modeled after the firefighting crews of the CCC.

The National Park Service was in charge of administering the CCC in Chiricahua National Monument, while the U.S. Army provided enrollees with food, clothing, shelter, education and discipline in the camp and was tasked with the construction, administration and medical care of each camp. The U.S. Forest Service was in charge of the actual projects. The Office of Education provided education to the enrollees, including tools to hone the skills of multiple trades.

Each camp consisted of four wood-frame barracks capable of holding fifty men each and quarters for U.S. Army and Forest Service personnel, a mess hall, a kitchen, a headquarters building, an infirmary, latrines, garages and tool and supply houses. Enrollees worked eight-hour days five days a week, rising at 6:00 a.m. CCC enrollees were involved in firefighting efforts and building and staffing fire lookouts in the Chiricahua Mountains. Many of the buildings they created were from rock quarried on the south side of the Chiricahua Mountains. This allowed the buildings to adhere to the appearance of the natural environment.

Several prominent camps established in the Chiricahua Mountains included Bonita Canyon Camp (NM-2), Cave Creek Camp (F-10-A), Rucker Canyon Camp (F-12-A) and Turkey Creek Camp (F-47-A). CCC camp designations in the Chiricahua Mountains were labeled "F," indicating that the camp was assigned to the U.S. Forest Service, or "NM," indicative that the camp was affiliated with the National Park Service, including the national monument. Cave Creek Camp (F-10-A), located on the east side of the Chiricahua Mountains near the town of Portal, operated from June 1933 through the spring of 1942. During this time, the camp constructed the Portal Ranger Station Office, the Rustler Park Fire Guard Station and the South Fork Campground. The camp was formerly known as Camp Harold C. Riley, after one of its original enrollees who was killed in a blasting accident. A debris-filled culvert cave-in caused by a blasting accident on August 5, 1940, took the lives of three more of the camp's enrollees. Little remains of the camp today except for a stone garage that is currently occupied by the U.S. Forest Service.

Camp F-12-A was created on July 12, 1933, and lasted until the spring of 1941. Located in Rucker Canyon at an elevation of 5,500 feet, the camp was originally known as Camp Greenway after General John C. Greenway, a former Rough Rider and Arizona miner. Several adobe buildings were constructed, including a mess hall. Built on a hillside, the camp was operating at maximum capacity in 1935 with over two hundred men and a working radius of 125 square miles. Camp F-12-A built recreational areas, including Bathtub Park, Cypress Park, Hermitage Park, Rucker Park and Rustler Park.

The Portal Ranger Station was built by the CCC under the supervision of Camp Cave Creek (F-10-A). Its dimensions are thirty-four feet wide by fifteen feet long. The building materials used were wood with a riverbed rock veneer laid in mortar. Decorative half-timbers and riverbed rock are apparent from the front view. *Courtesy of United States Department of Agriculture.*

The camp was plagued with water issues, including dry wells. Water was imported from another site located six miles distant until new wells were dug after 1937 and additional rains resolved the problem. Water availability was an important factor in selecting the location of CCC camps.

Turkey Creek Camp (F-47-A) operated sporadically between 1935 and 1937. Located on the west side of the Chiricahua Mountains in Turkey Creek Canyon, this camp was involved with multiple building projects that included the erection of the Cima Park Fire Guard Station and the Fly Peak Fire Lookout and the establishment of campgrounds at Fly Peak and Rustler Park. Views from atop the Fly Peak Fire Lookout were commanding, ranging from Cochise Head to the north down to Chiricahua Peak to the south. The Fly Peak Fire Lookout was later removed in 1971. Named after Camillus S. Fly, a renowned Tombstone pioneer and photographer, Fly Peak attains a height of 9,759 feet in the middle of the Chiricahua Mountains.

Bonita Canyon Camp (NM-2), located in the Chiricahua National Monument, operated from the summer of 1934 through the summer of 1939. It closed the following June, and the buildings were given to Lillian and Ed Riggs of nearby Faraway Ranch. It was located in Silver Spur Meadow in the Chiricahua National Monument. Administered by the National Park

Service, it was involved in multiple forest service projects in the northern Chiricahua Mountains. The camp did have its challenges, including issues with its septic system draining into the floodplain of Bonita Canyon. The Riggses, who owned Faraway Ranch and who obtained water from Bonita Creek, one mile from the site, complained about the effluent discharge from the CCC septic systems.

Today, the remains of the camp can be accessed by taking the Silver Spur Meadow Trail, a 1.2-mile trail beginning at the Faraway Ranch Picnic Area. Along the Silver Spur Meadow Trail are remnants of a mess hall built by the Civilian Conservation Corps. All that remains of the mess hall are the fireplace chimneys built by Camp NM-2. The building, along with the area encompassing sixty thousand acres of land, became part of the Silver Spur Guest Ranch that operated between 1948 and 1968. The ranch changed owners several times before it was sold to the National Park Service in 1967 by Ray and Ruth Kent. Afterward, the buildings were demolished, with only the foundations remaining.

The only intact structure created by the CCC enrollees is a rock bear cage that was built into the northern slope of Bonita Canyon. Two windows with iron bars protruding from a wall of mortared rocks at the cave face define what has become known as the Cima Bear Cage. This house contained their mascot, an orphaned black bear cub who was attracted to their camp because of his fondness for the men's shoes. The orphaned bear cub was adopted at the Coronado National Forest fly camp (Camp NM-2) in Cima Park. The bear was fed staples from the CCC's mess hall, including bottled milk. When the bear reached a size that proved challenging to manage, the camp designed a cage for its pet in 1936. Once the bear outgrew the rock cage, he was released into the wild at Barfoot Park. Today, the rock bear cage is the only intact structure remaining from the original camp.

The Civilian Conservation Corps had a solid history of contributions in the Chiricahua Mountains. The CCC camps in the Chiricahua Mountains were all involved in building miles of mountains roads, erosion barriers, stock tanks, rock terraces and fenced rangeland and the installment of waterline and telephone lines, as well as re-vegetation. Many of the camp buildings were temporary, consisting of frame construction and some of adobe. Canvas tents were used when working in remote locations. The CCC built log cabins along the Crest Trail under the direction of the Coronado National Forest. One such cabin was the Cima Cabin, built in 1933 to house summer firefighters. Although the U.S. Forest Service no longer uses the cabin, it is still used on occasion by fire and trail crews.

Above and below: It was the Civilian Conservation Corps that made needed improvements to the Chiricahua Mountains during the 1930s. The work crew seen here was used to erect fences, cattle guards, stock tanks and corrals. It was also involved in the re-vegetation of grasslands. The forest service enforced grazing restrictions by using CCC labor to erect fencing, cattle guards, corrals, stock tanks and restore overgrazed areas of grassland. Although the relationship between the forest service and ranchers was at times tense, the ranchers began to accept grazing regulations as a means of allowing former overgrazed allotments to regenerate and improve the health of their livestock. *Courtesy of Chiricahua National Monument.*

The Civilian Conservation Corps men are hard at work grading and implementing erosion control on Bonita Canyon Highway. *Courtesy of Chiricahua National Monument.*

A group of CCC workers from Bonita Canyon Camp (NM-2-A) poses for a picture on Bonita Canyon Highway. *Courtesy of Chiricahua National Monument.*

During the 1930s, the CCC constructed trails using dynamite. Evidence of powder magazines exists one hundred yards east of Bonita Canyon Highway. The importance of powder and cap magazines was to store dynamite and blasting caps in remote, isolated locations that remained dry and accessible for use. These powder magazines were encased with solid rock walls, with a dirt floor and a exterior vent along the surface of the slope. The encasement was accessible through a one-fourth-inch-thick steel door encased by a wooden frame and mortared into the surrounding rock.

Communication was necessary to maintain contact and sustain the integrity at all levels in the monument and the rest of the Chiricahua Mountains. Camp NM-2 constructed telephone lines that connected the Lookout Station atop Sugarloaf Mountain with the U.S. Forest Service Ranger Station in Portal and other communication points throughout the mountains. The phone line went out of use after the CCC was disbanded. By 1966, radio communications were the primary means of contact between all the localities in the monument and the ranger station in Portal.

By the start of World War II, desertions had increased among the CCC camps in the Chiricahua Mountains. Some of the men remained on the roster in the camp yet had secured employment outside the camp to supplement their income. By the end of the spring of 1942, the CCC

The Civilian Conservation Corps was responsible for the erection of the rock vista at Massai Point. *Courtesy of Chiricahua National Monument.*

The Civilian Conservation Corps was responsible for naming some of the prominent rock features in Chiricahua National Monument. The young men are holding signs pointing out the names of the rock formations that still exist today. Because the rock formations consist mainly of rhyolite, they are less likely to weather at the rate of sandstone. That is why rock formations at Chiricahua National Monument have retained their appearance for centuries, in contrast to the ever-changing appearance of the sandstone rock formations at Bryce's Canyon in Utah. *Courtesy of Chiricahua National Monument.*

had disbanded in the Chiricahua Mountains. The entire expenditure for CCC projects in the Chiricahua Mountains included $200,000 for a road and trail system, along with an additional $100,000 for building structures, laying pipes and directing water flow.

Chapter 9

Air Traffic

Air traffic over and around the Chiricahua Mountains has been a common event for at least the past seventy-five years. It is not uncommon for visitors in the Chiricahua Mountains to view commercial airliners flying overhead. However, there have been unfortunate instances of plane crashes in the flight pattern over the Chiricahua Mountains. Although not frequent, these crashes are well documented, including several that happened during World War II. Factors for these airplane crashes include lack of maneuverability and adverse weather conditions. Over the past decade, the sport of aerotrekking, which will be explained shortly, has become popular in southeastern Arizona and southwestern New Mexico. The Chiricahua Mountains have been a common place to view this sport.

Within the continental boundaries of the United States, 14,900 airmen lost their lives in six thousand fatal crashes involving military aircraft during World War II. One such instance happened on October 12, 1941, involving the final flight of Marine Corps flight sergeant Edward "Mac" McMahon and a Marine Corps Vought OS2U Kingfisher #5351 en route from New York to San Diego. The passengers included twenty-six-year-old navy radio operator Oscar Rohr, who was on leave to visit his wife in San Diego. Adverse weather conditions began to appear as the aircraft approached the Chiricahua Mountains. Thick cloudbanks obscured visibility. While flying up a sharp canyon near the town of Paradise, Flight Sergeant McMahon of the U.S. Marine Corps determined that he lacked the altitude necessary to clear the Chiricahua mountain range. He responded by banking his aircraft

The Vought OS2U Kingfisher seen in the air during World War II. *Courtesy of U.S. Navy National Museum of Naval Aviation.*

to the left in an attempt to reverse his course and retreat out of the canyon. Unfortunately, the left wing of the plane struck a tall juniper tree, causing the aircraft to crash into the mountainside. The aircraft later burst into flames, burning Sergeant McMahon to death. Oscar Rohr was catapulted from the craft, surviving with a broken nose. He was discovered two miles from the crash by Civilian Conservation Corps enrollees and provided a full account of the crash to Lieutenant Ira Bellinger, the Civilian Conservation Corps commandant. A later investigation concluded that had McMahon turned twenty feet earlier, he would have missed the large juniper tree. Today, remnants of the crash can still be found in the Chiricahua Mountains, including engine exhaust manifolds, engine throttle, hydraulic line and bomb shackle. An online account states that among the debris, Edward McMahon's USMC globe and anchor insignia was found and returned to his ninety-seven-year-old wife.

Several years after the Kingfisher crash, a military training flight from Douglas Army Airfield would meet disaster while flying over the Chiricahua Mountains. The flight consisted of three AT-17 "Bobcats," each with an instructor and pilot. They departed Douglas Army Airfield on December 28, 1943, for a test flight over the Chiricahua Mountains en route to Rodeo, New Mexico. While flying in the Chiricahua Mountains, a strong downdraft prevented the aircraft from attaining the necessary altitude to clear a ridge in Price Canyon. Two aircraft crashed into the side of the canyon, killing two out of four men. The third aircraft made it over the top of the ridge but clipped the trees and brush, causing it to stall and crash into the face of Sage Peak, killing both pilots, Second Lieutenant Robert Andrus and Cadet Gayle Kral. The two survivors of the previous crash did not know the whereabouts of the third AT-17. It eluded the United States Army Air Force until a hunter stumbled on the remains of it in September 1945. The remains at the crash site include one of the seven-cylinder Jacobs 225-horsepower engines, along with parts of the steel frames of the fuselage and wings. Sage Peak was named for ranger Harley H. Sage, who died in the service on November 13, 1918.

Another incident in the Chirichaua Mountains involved two brothers who survived a crash in their single-engine Cessna 182 while scouting for deer in the Chiricahua Mountains in November 1990. The culprit behind the crash was lack of room to maneuver, forcing the pilot to conduct a crash landing. Robert Rowe, a methods analyst for the American Telegraph and Telephone Company, and his brother Carl Rowe, a building contractor, walked sixteen miles through rugged terrain before they were rescued four days after the crash. Both suffered broken bones, including broken wrists. Robert Rowe also suffered a broken foot. Adverse weather conditions slowed the search with snow and rain along with nighttime temperature below freezing. Streams provided the men with water. The Rowes were in the early stages of hypothermia and had been hallucinating, seeing children walking around in front of them, when they were finally rescued. Another recent crash in the Chiricahua Mountains involved a single-engine home-built Thorp T-18 on the morning of August 26, 2010. Both people onboard were killed. The circumstances involving the crash remain unknown, according to Ian Gregor of the Federal Aviation Administration (FAA). The crash occurred in a remote area of the Chiricahua Mountains and was witnessed from afar.

The Chiricahua Mountains, along with the surrounding deserts and playas, are rapidly becoming a popular place for aerotrekking for several reasons, including their remoteness, weather and their lack of high commercial air traffic. Aerotrekking involves personal aircraft that fly several hundred feet above the ground at speeds between 25 and 115 miles per hour (depending on the model), and they have the ability to cover a range of 300 miles. These flying craft allow people greater accessibility to localities whose rugged terrain makes them inaccessible by foot or car. Flying over the tops of ponderosa pines or the magnificent rock formations found in the Chiricahua Mountains and elsewhere in southeastern Arizona is an awe-inspiring adventure. Classified as "light sports aircraft," aerotrekking planes require special licensing from the FAA because of its restrictions against the flying of ultra-light aircraft within the boundaries of urban areas and within 30 miles surrounding commercial airports. The aircraft are described as resembling motorcycles with ultra-light wings. A propeller in the rear powers the craft while it is controlled by a steering bar at the pilot's fingertips.

The Bootheel of New Mexico, along with the Chiricahua Mountains, has captivated ultra-light pilots over the past decade. The surrounding valleys experience over three hundred days of cobalt blue skies and sunshine each year. However, during certain times of the year, the area experiences gusts of wind in excess of 15 miles per hour, prohibiting aerotrekking. John McAfee and other like-minded airmen organized a group known as the Sky Gypsies, named for their penchant for flying unconventional aircraft. John McAfee, a software entrepreneur known for antivirus applications who at one time was worth over $100 million, owned 157 acres of real estate in Rodeo, New Mexico. He bought the property in 2004, investing $11.5 million into an infrastructure that would accommodate his passion for aerotrekking. That infrastructure included a series of remote airstrips along a 1,100-mile circuit in southeastern Arizona and southern New Mexico. Rodeo, New Mexico, was selected as a base of operations because of its Amigos del Cielo Airport. Lack of air traffic over that particular area also made it attractive. McAfee built a general store, the Sky Gypsy Café and several hangars for his aerotrekking business. The property even included a movie theater. The business was short-lived, and the economic downturn in 2009 forced him to sell his property at auction for $1.15 million.

Chapter 10

Wildfire History

The Chiricahua Mountains have endured wildfires for millions of years. Until recently, many of these wildfires were sparked by lightning strikes, as has been determined by use of dendrochronological techniques applied to tree ring samples dating back to 1644. Fire season in southeastern Arizona correlates with the drier and hotter months that occur between April and October. Although rain comes in the form of a monsoon in July and August, the dry conditions that precede the rain often include lightning strikes and high winds. The essential ingredients to fueling a high-intensity fire include low moisture levels, low humidity, high winds and high temps. Additional lightning strikes also increase the likelihood of fire once the monsoon begins. Recent wildfires in the Chiricahua Mountains have caused severe scarring to the scenic landscape, and they continue to have far-reaching consequences for both aesthetics and safety, as landslides are caused by erosion that occurs with decreased tree stability in the region.

Studies regarding tree ring–based fire history in the Chiricahua Mountains have attempted to find a correlation between heightened fire activity and the Apache presence in the Chiricahua Mountains, contrasted to fewer fires prior and after their inhabitancy in the mountain ranges. There is a possible association between Apache and fire occurrence in the Chiricahua Mountains, although few eyewitness accounts are available for Apache-made wildfires. What is known is that the Apache used fire to drive game, increase forage for livestock and large game, as a tool for direct and indirect warfare tactics and as a means of creating favorable travel corridors. Fire occurrence increased between 1760 and 1786, when the Apache waged war against the Spanish. Fires decreased after 1786 once peace was established between the warring parties. Recorded wildfires in Arizona between 1860 and 1890 were more numerous and larger than those during the twentieth century. This was due in part to an increase in the grazing of cattle coupled with a greater attempt at fire suppression. Oak woodlands in canyon bottoms helped the spread of fire in the Chiricahua Mountain Range between the pine forest in the higher elevations and the lower grasslands. Often times, lightning was the culprit.

Although fewer in number, more intense fires occurred in the Chiricahua Mountains by the early twentieth century. This reduction in number was caused by additional fire suppression efforts by the U.S. government and locals along with increased grazing by cattle. The effects of cattle grazing reduced the availability of grassland that was once abundant prior to 1890 and more susceptible to causing larger wildfires. Selective logging practices conducted in the Chiricahua Mountains from the late nineteenth century through the mid-twentieth century helped thin the trees and the undergrowth of wood

The barren patch of land on the left is the site of a sawmill that was once operated by the Riggs family and later the Sweeney family. The view is of Barfoot Park looking out toward the distant Sulphur Springs Valley. Ida Peak is at the center with Barfoot Peak at the right. A framed ranger station was also located in the vicinity of the sawmill. *Courtesy of William Ascarza.*

During the late nineteenth century, the Chiricahua Mountains were logged to support mining interests, such as Bisbee in southeastern Arizona. Logging continued through the middle of the twentieth century. Practices such as this helped remove underbrush and dead trees that could potentially add fuel to a forest fire. *Courtesy of United States Department of Agriculture.*

and brush that contribute to the spread and severity of wildfires. The use of sawmills in strategic areas throughout the Chiricahua Mountains in the late nineteenth and early twentieth centuries helped remove patches of trees that would otherwise have been prone to the spark of a match or a bolt of lightning. One such sawmill was located in West Turkey Creek in the 1880s. It was established for the purpose of providing local timber to the mines in Tombstone and Bisbee. It was along Rock Creek Trail that several sawmills were in operation due to the abundance of fir trees useful for the timber support in the underground mines. One sawmill operator, a man by the name of Morse, christened the stream Turkey Creek after the abundance of wild turkeys in the area. Another sawmill operation in Pinery Canyon, close to the Methodist Church Camp, was operated by Major Downing around 1900. Both it and the sawmill that operated in Rustler Park during the 1940s and 1950s helped reduce the amount of undergrowth, enabling a healthier strand of pine tree to grow while reducing the fire hazard.

In addition to challenges posed by funding and forest management, fire suppression in southeastern Arizona has led to high-intensity wildfires.

Heightened efforts at fire suppression in the twentieth century enabled vegetation to grow in size and density, obscuring some views in the Chiricahua Mountains. These practices led to buildup of fire-burning material during severe drought conditions. The Rattlesnake Fire occurring in June and July 1994 was the largest fire to burn in the Chiricahua Mountains in a century. It burned 27,500 acres of forest in the Chiricahua Mountains. The Wallow Fire that occurred around the same time as the Horseshoe 2 Fire has been, at this writing, the largest forest fire in the recorded history of Arizona. Originating in the White Mountains of Arizona on May 29, 2011, and lasting until July 8, 2011, the Wallow Fire burned 817 square miles (522,900 acres) in eastern Arizona and 24 square miles (15,000 acres) in western New Mexico.

The Horseshoe 2 Fire ignited in Horseshoe Canyon on the southeastern flank of the Chiricahua Mountains. This manmade fire began on May 8, 2011, consuming 9,000 acres the first day. Total containment was not reached until June 25, when 222,954 acres had burned. The fire ranked as the fourth-largest fire in Arizona history. Total cost to suppress the Horseshoe 2 Fire exceeded $50 million, including 1,379 personnel, 38 crews, 66 engines, 9 helicopters, 3 heavy air tankers, 3 heavy helitankers and 4 bulldozers. Twenty-three structures were lost to the fire. The firefighters were challenged in battling the flames because of the steep terrain and dry conditions that prevailed.

The prospects for a high-intensity wildfire such as the Horseshoe 2 Fire were increased by a severe freeze in February 2010 that killed many trees, shrubs and cacti. This provided additional fuel that combined with the low moisture in the air and enhanced the burning of the soil during the Horseshoe 2 Fire. Heat from the fire was so intense that is melted a guardrail along the Bonita Canyon Highway. Some of the effects from the Horseshoe 2 Fire include open or exposed routes used by illegal immigration and drug smuggling, massive loss of wildlife and water holes and springs filled with sedimentation and ash caused by debris flow and erosion. However, one positive aspect might be found in the destruction by the fire of many of the bark beetles that inhabited the trees in the Chiricahua Mountains. Bark beetles have caused pine trees in the Chiricahua Mountains to yellow and die.

One can view the impact of the Horseshoe 2 Fire by walking the Echo Canyon Trail in the Chiricahua National Monument and driving the first half of the recently graded Pinery Canyon Road on 17.9 miles of unpaved path beginning near the entrance of Chiricahua National Monument and ending by the Southwestern Research Station on the east side of the Chiricahua Mountains. The frequency of flash floods in this area is directly related to the scope and magnitude of the wildfire. Lack of vegetation that at one time kept the soil in place led to erosion without the constraints of a stabilizing barrier. Areas of most concern for flash flooding include West Whitetail Basin, the Visitors' Center at Chiricahua National Monument, Faraway Ranch, Paradise, East Turkey Basin, Cave Creek and Portal.

Although the Horseshoe 2 Fire was the most severe in recorded history in the Chiricahua Mountains, it did not completely destroy the mountain

Seen inside the confines of the Sugarloaf Mountain Lookout is an Osborn fire finder that was invented by U.S. Forest Service engineer William B. Osborne in 1911. This instrument saw use in many fire lookouts across the country. *Courtesy of William Ascarza.*

A hand-drawn cigarette pokes out of Smokey the Bear's mouth along Forest Road 74E in Rucker Canyon. This image, taken in the summer of 2009, would prove an ominous sign for future events in the Chiricahua Mountains. Two years later, the Horseshoe 2 Fire would become the most destructive fire in modern history in the Chiricahua Mountains, affecting 80 percent of the mountain range. *Courtesy of William Ascarza.*

The Horseshoe 2 Fire originated in Horseshoe Canyon. Caused by humans, it is one of the unfortunate results of illegal immigration and drug running that has blighted the land. *Courtesy of William Ascarza.*

range. Despite a large amount of mixed conifer, oak brush, pinyon, juniper, ponderosa pine and grasses adversely affected, the fire burned a mosaic pattern across the mountains, sparing large sections of green space. Grasses, flowers and green treetops have made a return. Signs of recovery include soil regeneration and new growth emerging from the old growth. The areas around Faraway Ranch, Cave Creek and Camp Rucker were relatively untouched from the ravages of the fire. While Onion Saddle, Barfoot Park and Rustler Park were hit hard by fire, Lower Cave Creek Canyon survived the fire relatively unscathed. Monsoon rains have helped the minor damage

DD Gamble Guest Lodge lies between the Chiricahua and the Peloncillo Mountains on the Arizona–New Mexico border at the gateway to Horseshoe Canyon. Tom and Alicia Davidson are excellent hosts with a wealth of knowledge about the local land. A visit to the ranch provides options of bird-watching, miniature horse carriage driving, trail riding, hiking, climbing and night sky observing. *Courtesy of William Ascarza.*

The Horseshoe 2 Fire as seen looking northeast while driving on Highway 80, ten miles west of Douglas, Arizona, on May 30, 2011. The Chiricahua Mountains take on the distant appearance of a volcanic eruption. The fire lasted from May 8 until it was 100 percent contained on June 25, 2011. *Courtesy of William Ascarza.*

Seen several years after the Horseshoe 2 Fire, water from Horsheshoe Canyon continues to channel debris from the worst fire in modern Chiricahua Mountain history. *Courtesy of William Ascarza.*

to heal in a short time. Hiking trails that suffered severe damage include Inspiration Point and Echo Park. However, the upper section of Echo Canyon Trail and Heart of Rocks suffered minor damage. Repairing the stability of the damaged trails has been undertaken through the Burned Area Emergency Response (BAER) funding using the Southwest Conservation Corps. The acres broken down by ownership that were affected by the fire included 13,934 acres of private land, 2,874 acres of state land, 192,647 acres of forest service land and 1,336 acres belonging to the Bureau of Land Management. Of the affected land, 27,730 acres, the equivalent of 12.4 percent of the area, were affected by a high burn severity, another 66,226 acres (29.7 percent) were affected by a moderate burn, another 84,852 acres (38.0 percent) were affected by a low burn and a remaining 44,146 acres (19.8 percent) remained unchanged by the fire.

According to official reports, the fire was cause by humans. Among the locals and certain authorities, there is a consensus that it was started by illegal immigrants. Debate continues to rage regarding the efforts made by the U.S. Forest Service to put out the fire. Controlled back burning and the destruction of private property, wildlife and vegetation occurred throughout the mountain range during the life of the Horseshoe 2 Fire. In the aftermath, concerns arouse about the number of sandbags used to prevent erosion. Lessons learned from the disastrous consequences of the Horseshoe 2 Fire include the importance of frequent, low-temperature fires during the life cycle of a forest. These unsuppressed fires maintain healthy vegetation while removing the buildup of fuels such as dry timber that can easily ignite in a fire. With increasing droughts and excess vegetation and surface debris, the threat of high-intensity fires in mountain ranges in the western United States is certain.

Chapter 11

Wildlife

Wildlife in the Chiricahua Mountains is both abundant and diverse. From the calls of the distinctive blue- and gray-feathered Mexican jays to the curiosity of the black bears and stealth of the mountain lions, the rugged terrain of the Chiricahua Mountains has traditionally supported a vast mountain woodland that provides sustenance and shelter. While black bears are not numerous in the Chiricahua Mountains, they do exist and are active year round. Mexican raccoon and coatimundi are found along West Turkey Creek. Bobcat, mountain lion and coyote are always in search of a quick meal in the form of Coues white-tailed deer.

The Chiricahua Mountains are considered one of the most diverse areas for birds, insects, mammals and reptiles. They are host to animals that are also found in the Sierra Madre Mountains of Mexico. These include the Apache fox squirrel and the Mexican chickadee. The Chiricahua fox squirrel, a subspecies of the Mexican fox squirrel, appears red and is rather uncommon in the Chiricahua Mountains. However, it is confined exclusively in the United States to the Chiricahua Mountains. The diverse diet of the Chiricahua fox squirrel includes pine nuts, fungi, bark, acorns and mistletoe berries. Populations of black speckled and rainbow trout have been documented in the upper parts of Cave Creek and Rucker Canyon. The jaguarondi—a small, mysterious, rare cat—is also thought to inhabit the Chiricahua Mountains.

The Chiricahua Mountains are a world-class birding destination for breeding species, as well as migrants and wintering species. Almost 50 percent of all the bird species found in the United States inhabit this range. The densest known raptor population in the United States occurs in Cave Creek Canyon, with a total of twenty-four species actively nesting in the locality. Cave Creek Canyon, located on the northeast side of the Chiricahua Mountains, includes eleven species of owls. The Chiricahua Mountains are the northern limit of the elegant trogon and Mexican chickadee. Birders flock in numbers to visit the Chiricahua Mountains during the spring migration of songbirds as they journey north. South Fork Cave Creek is the premier area for bird-watching in the Chiricahua Mountains. The Chiricahua Mountains are home to over 370 species of birds, including 14 types of hummingbirds, and 60 types of butterflies.

The Chiricahua Mountains have been the home of the thick-billed parrot, Gould's turkey, Mexican spotted owl, elegant trogon and sulphur-bellied flycatchers. The Mexican spotted owl and elegant trogon nest in sycamore-lined riparian canyons. The elegant trogon (formerly known as the coppery-tailed trogon), the painted redstart and red-faced warbler are among the many birds found in the Cave Creek area. Rare birds include the Mexican chickadee, which, within the United States, only breeds in the Chiricahua Mountains and the nearby Animas Mountains to the east in New Mexico. Pinery Canyon is the only documented nesting site in the United States outside of Florida for the short-tailed hawk. Peregrine falcons and Chihuahuan ravens also visit the range.

Three species of quail inhabit the Chiricahua Mountains, including the Montezuma quail, Gambel's quail and Mearns quail. Montezuma quail and Mearns quail inhabit the grasses dispersed among the Madrean oak woodland habitat between 5,000 and 8,000 feet. Gambel's quail are the most common quail in Arizona and are found below 5,500 feet in the mesquite grasslands and desert.

Thick-billed parrots may have never been full-time residents in the United States. However, there are published accounts of their existence in southeastern Arizona from the 1890s through 1938, when the last thick-billed parrot was spotted in the wild in the Chiricahua Mountains. Pinery Canyon and Rucker Canyon were popular spots for sightings of thick-billed parrots. Padre Francisco Kino reported seeing caged thick-billed parrots in the early 1700s during his visitation to the villages of the Pima Indians along the Gila River. Their main breeding area is located south of the border in the Sierra Madre Occidental. Because of their bright green coloration with a red head and black beak and a noisy demeanor, they most assuredly gave away their position to natural predators such as the northern goshawk.

They can be heard several miles away. During the early twentieth century, U.S. soldiers and local residents used the parrots as target practice, which inevitably was a factor that led to their demise in the Chiricahua Mountains.

Between 1986 and 1993, efforts to reintroduce thick-billed parrots to Arizona were ineffective. Eighty-eight birds, many of which were confiscated from smugglers, were released into the wild in southeastern Arizona. Some flew as far north as Payson during the summer, establishing a brief home in the Mogollon Rim 250 miles north of the Chiricahua Mountains before returning to the Chiricahua Mountains in the winter. However, a mixture of drought-devastated pine crops and predation by the northern goshawks proved their ultimate demise. Estimates have been made that more than three thousand thick-billed parrots exist in the wild in Mexico. These wild birds are more adept at survival then the captive-bred birds because of their proclivity to forage for food in flocks rather than solo. This method is also helpful against natural predators, such as northern goshawks and red-tailed hawks. Mexico has established laws against capturing the birds and moving them elsewhere. The United States has since partnered with Mexico to help sustain its population of thick-billed parrots, which currently nest fifty miles south of the border within visibility of the Chiricahua Mountains. It is possible that this cooperation may prompt the Mexican government to coordinate efforts with the United States government to lure future populations of thick-billed parrots to migrate north into the Chiricahua Mountains.

Gould's turkeys have been reintroduced recently to the Chiricahua Mountains. One of only two wild turkey subspecies that occur in Arizona, the other being Merriam's turkeys, they were at one time common in riparian areas and isolated mountain ranges in southeastern Arizona. Their numbers greatly decreased as southeastern Arizona became populated by settlers, who hunted the wild turkeys as a food source, causing their disappearance by the 1920s. Over the past decade, cooperative efforts between the Arizona Game and Fish Department, National Wild Turkey Federation, U.S. Forest Service and Mexican government have successfully reintroduced Gould's turkeys to many of the larger mountain ranges in southeastern Arizona. Several hundred of these birds are now believed to reside in the Chiricahua Mountains.

Found in the Chiricahua Mountains year round due to the mild climate, the Mexican spotted owl is considered a federally threatened species in Arizona. The Chiricahua Mountains provide many canyons and unique rock formations, along with dense patches of vegetation, that provide excellent nesting opportunities for this owl. The owl feeds on bats, lizards and small rodents. The call of the Mexican spotted owl is a *whoo, hoo-hoo, hoooo*. The Mexican spotted owl is a subspecies of the spotted owl.

The pink-winged moth, a new species of moth discovered in southeastern Arizona, was first discovered by a biologist in the Chiricahua Mountains around Onion Saddle. It was attracted to a sheet illuminated by a mercury vapor lamp. A subsequent DNA test proved this moth to be a new species that was probably discovered due to overwintering.

The Chiricahua Mountains are also host to several species of rattlesnakes whose main source of prey are rodents. The twin-spotted and banded-rock rattlesnakes are such examples that occur in the higher elevations. Additional examples include blacktail and diamondback rattlesnakes. The twin-spotted rattlesnake is both rare and active during the year and reaches an average length of two feet. Considered pit vipers, their favorite meal is lizards, and their most prevalent locality in the Chiricahua Mountains is Barfoot Park.

The Chiricahua leopard frog continues to face challenges to its survival because of the introduction of non-native species of predators, including bullfrogs, mosquitofish, tiger salamander and bluegill sunfish. Once prevalent in numbers up until the 1970s, the species has undergone a significant population decline over the past several decades. Today, many of the remaining populations of the Chiricahua leopard frog are found in stock ponds that last for an ephemeral amount of time. The 1980s saw a brief resurgence in numbers due to abundant rainfall, allowing small ponds of water lacking predators to accrue. The Chiricahua leopard frog is a federally threatened species. Locations frequented by Chiricahua leopard frogs in the Chiricahua Mountains include Herb Martyr and John Hands Dams, West Turkey Creek, Rucker Canyon, Cave Creek, South Fork and Portal.

Sandhill cranes in a V-shaped pattern of flight. A long-legged, long-neck, gray bird, the sandhill crane can attain a height of four feet and spread its wings up to seven feet. A record 40,499 wintering sandhill cranes visited the Sulphur Springs Valley in 2010. Sandhill cranes can fly one hundred miles in a single day in their search for food. *Courtesy of William Ascarza.*

An acorn woodpecker, seen here, is a common inhabitant in the oak woodlands of the Chiricahua Mountains. *Courtesy of William Ascarza.*

Born and raised on a ranch in the southern end of the Chiricahua Mountains, Warner Glenn has had the rare opportunity of sighting jaguars in the wild on two separate occasions, once in 1996 and again in 2006. His published photography of these encounters has awakened people to the plight of a cat that many thought no longer roamed freely in the boundaries of the United States. At one time, jaguars roamed as far north as the Grand Canyon. Encouraged hunting in Arizona by the Bureau of Biological Survey beginning in 1918 caused fewer and fewer sightings throughout the twentieth century. The last known female jaguar in the United States was killed in the Apache National Forest in southeastern Arizona in 1963.

Chapter 12

Willcox Playa

Today, as one travels from Tucson to the Chiricahua Mountains, the Willcox Playa seen along the way is a distinct feature in the Sulphur Springs Valley. The valley itself stretched one hundred miles from north to south and twenty-five miles east to west. Composed of roaming dust devils on a windy day, the white outline of the Willcox Playa is evident from atop Sugarloaf Mountain in the Chiricahua Mountains. Temperatures on the Willcox Playa average between 29 degrees in the winter up to 105 degrees in the summer. Rainfall is more common in the summer, with an annual precipitation count of twelve inches.

The Willcox Playa, a dry lakebed located 30 miles northwest of the Chiricahua Mountains, dates back to the ice age, when it contained over forty feet of water and spanned a distance of 140 square miles fifteen thousand years ago. It is the deepest point of what was once an ancient lake known to locals as Lake Cochise. Lake Cochise existed during the Pleistocene era, when the climate was wetter. A freshwater lake that ran southward into Mexico, it eventually dried up due to climate change. Today, its remnants support ephemeral pools of water up to several inches in depth caused by excessive rainfall and snow from the runoff in the adjacent mountain ranges. The water quickly evaporates from exposure to the sun, leaving behind layers of alkaline deposits. This 8-mile-wide by 10-mile-long dry lake is the largest interior-draining basin in Arizona. It contains sediments that eroded from the Chiricahua Mountains, Dos Cabezas Mountains and Pinaleño Mountains. The sediments contain clay, mud, calcite, halite and gypsum. Fossils of horses and mammoths have been uncovered from the lake sediment. Meteorites have also been found in its confines surrounded by stabilized dune fields held together by grasses, indicating the former shoreline of the freshwater lake.

The Willcox Playa appears deceptive from the sky. A case in point occurred during World War II, when two navy fliers were transporting a flying boat across the country. They mistook the playa for a body of water and had a rough landing. Fragments of military hardware have been uncovered from the dry lake dating back to when the area was a test site used as a World War II bombing range. The alkaline surface of the dry lake covered up shrapnel and other metallic components when it was used as a practice run during the war. Some of the ordnance remains undetonated, and extreme caution should be undertaken when exploring the Willcox Playa. The periphery of the Willcox Playa includes sand dunes that are stabilized from the wind by grasses and shrubs, including alkalai sacaton, salt bush and mesquite.

Parts of the Willcox Playa are available for visitation during birding and wildlife viewing. The Willcox Playa Wildlife Area encompasses 595

The Willcox Playa, with a vantage point looking east toward the Dos Cabezas Mountains, is a popular spot to view sandhill cranes. It measures eight miles wide by ten miles long. Originally known as Lake Cochise, it extended twenty miles wide by eleven miles long, having a depth of thirty-five feet. The lake dried up over ten thousand years ago, and the lakebed is readily apparent today south of Interstate 10 west of Willcox. *Courtesy of William Ascarza.*

acres located seven miles south of Willcox. It is managed by Arizona Game and Fish Department and is a popular site for birders, who seek out the hundreds of bird species that visit this locality, including shorebirds, Swainson's hawk, black-necked stilt and wintering sandhill cranes. Every year between mid-October and mid-March, an average of twenty thousand sandhill cranes migrate to the Willcox Playa to roost and occupy. They are attracted by the availability of crops grown in the Sulphur Springs Valley, including corn, chilies, oats and wheat. Sometimes one can spot several hundred to several thousand cranes walking on the playa or around the nearby power plant ponds. The popularity of bird-watching in this area brought about the Wings Over Willcox Festival sponsored by the Willcox Chamber of Commerce, held every year in the third week of January. The festival includes guided bird-watching, along with natural and regional history tours, craft shows and hiking.

Chapter 13

Trails

One of the great assets of the Chiricahua Mountains is accessibility. Several hundred miles of trails exist in the Chiricahua Mountains maintained by both the U.S. Forest Service and the National Park Service. Some of the principal recreational areas in the Chiricahua Mountains include Cave Creek Canyon, Rucker Canyon and Bonita Canyon. Until the 1930s, the Chiricahua Mountains proved cumbersome to navigate. It was the Civilian Conservation Corps and rancher Ed Riggs, employed by the National Park Service as the trail foreman in Chiricahua National Monument, that led to the development of the Chiricahua Mountain trail system. The numerous trails found both in the national monument and throughout the Chiricahua Wilderness area enable hikers to visit the many pristine sites and wonders that this mountain range has to offer, including access to many of the unique rock formations. Access to the Chiricahaua Mountains proved challenging until roads and trail systems were established beginning in the 1920s. Many hiking trails throughout the Chiricahua Mountains follow drainage patterns. At present, Chiricahua National Monument consists of eighteen miles of day-use hiking trails.

The act of building trails was a challenging one due to the natural terrain of the mountain range. Not only was a skilled crew needed to successfully conduct the operation, but there was also mapping, surveying and blasting of the actual trail itself. Landscaping and rockwalling the trail would also need to be done after it had been created. However, first and foremost was a need to determine the length and grade of the road.

Many trails in Chiricahua National Monument were built by the Civilian Conservation Corps. The upper Rhyolite Canyon Trail, completed in November 1936, provides accessibility to the Echo Canyon, Ed Riggs and Hailstone Trails. Lower Rhyolite Canyon Trail, built by CCC Camp NM-2-A, was completed in December 1934. Beginning in the parking lot east of the visitor center at an elevation of 5,400 feet, it connects with the Upper Rhyolite Canyon and Sarah Deming Trails. The Silver Spur Meadow Trail is 1.2 miles in length beginning at the Faraway Ranch Picnic Area. It includes sights such as the Stafford Cabin and the remnants of Civilian Conservation Corps Camp NM-2-A.

The Echo Canyon Trail and the Ed Riggs Trail were completed by the CCC in 1936. They proved to be some of the most challenging tasks that Ed Riggs had undertaken during his tenure as a trail foreman. Echo Canyon was both narrow and treacherous. Despite the claim made by several mining engineers about the impossibility of building a trail in the area, Ed Riggs believed it could be done. Riggs worked under the threat of the superintendent of Southwestern National Monument that if he failed to successfully implement the trail, his job would be terminated. The completion of the Echo Canyon Trail was considered by Ed Riggs to be his greatest accomplishment. On his grave site, an inscription states that his

The appearance of a massive organ pipe formation is not out of the ordinary in the vast and intricate rock formations in the Chiricahua Mountains. *Courtesy of William Ascarza.*

Taffoni, seen here along the Echo Canyon Trail, is a scene depicting rock weathering. The Corsican word *taffoni* means "windows," or it could also come from *tafonare*, which means "to perforate." It defines the honeycomb weathering seen in this rhyolite formation along the trail. It also occurs in other types of rocks, including granite and sandstone in both humid and desert environments, whether cold or hot. *Courtesy of William Ascarza.*

masterpiece of engineering was the construction of the Echo Canyon Trail. The 1.6-mile Sarah Deming Trail, named for Sarah Deming Canyon, was built in March 1937. Sarah Deming was an out-of-state visitor who, on a visit with Ed Riggs to view Big Balanced Rock, slipped and fell, tearing a hole in the seat of her pants. Martha Riggs, Ed's aunt, offered the visitor an apron to cover the hole.

Natural Bridge Trail runs a length of 4.8 miles round trip. It covers an elevation beginning at 5,560 feet and climbing up to 5,980 feet. The trailhead is located 0.5 miles east of the campground on Bonita Canyon Scenic Drive. The trail is named for a water-carved bridge composed of exfoliating layers of rhyolite found at the end of the trail. The view of this unique wonder in Chiricahua National Monument is seen from an overlook. The natural bridge spans 37 feet in length and 26 feet in height. Both the Natural Bridge and Sugarloaf Trails were constructed as a means of fire suppression. The 0.8-mile, mostly level Hailstone Trail was aptly named for the spherulites

The water-carved Natural Bridge as seen from the 4.8-mile round-trip Natural Bridge Trail appears flush with surrounding vegetation. This is considered to be the least-used trail in the monument. It ascends through oak and juniper woodlands to a ridge and descends into a forest of Apache pine in Picket Park. The trail ends at an overlook where one can view the natural bridge across the canyon. *Courtesy of William Ascarza.*

that are evident along the western end on the trail. The spherulites appear like white hailstones that have weathered out of the tuff.

The Sugarloaf Mountain Trail is 1.8 miles round trip. Sugarloaf Mountain is 7,310 feet. The trail to the lookout atop Sugarloaf Mountain was constructed by the CCC in 1934 and completed in April the following year. Landslides are a problem that affects the Sugarloaf Mountain Trail. The composition of a white-gray layer of ash amid the welded rhyolite tuff tends to become unstable during years with substantial rainfall. It then becomes easily dislodged and travels down the slope of the mountain, inevitably causing trail damage. One of the more recent cases of this occurrence happened in 2001 and resulted in a temporary closure of the trail by the Park Service.

The Heart of Rocks–Echo Canyon Trail provides the hiker with spectacular views of rugged ash-flow tuff rocky terrain. This 7.3-mile round-trip trail loop located in the Chiricahua National Monument ranges in elevation between 5,400 feet and 6,860 feet. Rock formations found within the perimeter of the Heart of Rocks include Duck on a Rock, Thor's

Sugarloaf Mountain contains some of the youngest rock in the monument. This rock is known as dacite caprock and forms a dark-colored mesa atop Sugarloaf Mountain. The dacite is the result of a lava flow that occurred from the higher elevated slopes farther south during volcanic activity twenty-seven million years ago. Over time, the lava cooled, solidifying and forming a valley that has eroded, leaving the top of Sugarloaf Mountain as a lone remnant. *Courtesy of William Ascarza.*

Camel's Head is another example of an aptly named rock formation. *Courtesy of National Park Service Harpers Ferry Center Collections.*

Opposite, bottom: The Sugarloaf Fire Lookout was completed by the CCC in June 1935. Dynamite was used to excavate the base of the lookout, and the lower four feet of lookout walls were constructed from the rock excavated from the blasting. The Sugarloaf Fire Lookout history of reporting fire and lightning strikes includes the use of carrier pigeons, heliographs, radio and telephone. An operational fire lookout included a fire finder, kitchen, work area and sleeping area. Historic fire lookouts in the Chiricahua Mountains include the Sugarloaf Mountain lookout and the Monte Vista fire lookout, built in 1916. The Barfoot Lookout was consumed by the Horseshoe 2 Fire. *Courtesy of William Ascarza.*

Yet another rock formation of rhyolite with a surface coating of green lichen is the obvious Duck on a Rock. *Courtesy of William Ascarza.*

Hammer, Punch and Judy, Pinnacle Balanced Rock and Camel's Head. Unlike many of the other trails in the Chiricahua Mountains designed for both horseback riding and hiking, the Heart of Rocks Trail was designed specifically for hiking.

The Inspiration Point Trail is one of the most spectacular and challenging trails found in the monument. Beginning at the juncture of the Mushroom Rock and Big Balanced Rock Trails, the trail follows a distance of one-half mile, averaging over seven thousand feet in elevation. Impressive views of Lower Bonita Canyon, Rhyolite Canyon and Sulphur Springs Valley mark the highlight of the trail, constructed by Ed Riggs between 1923 and 1934. Upon hiking the trail to Inspiration Point, a fantastic view awaits of the Sulphur Springs Valley and the Dragoon Mountains.

Constructed in 1932 by the U.S. Forest Service (USFS) and the Bureau of Public Roads, the scenic eight-mile Bonita Canyon Highway, also known as Bonita Canyon Drive, begins at the entrance of the monument to the higher elevations of over 6,650 feet found at Echo Canyon, Massai Point and the Sugarloaf Mountain Trailhead. Bonita Canyon itself was viewed by the Apache as a trade route connecting east from west. Automobile pull-out points along Bonita Canyon Highway were established in 1960 so that visitors had a safe opportunity for taking pictures of the unique rhyolite rock formations such as China Boy, Organ Pipe and Sea Captain.

Massai Point is one of the most popular places to visit in the Chiricahua National Monument because of its ease of accessibility. Designed by the Bureau of Public Roads in 1932, it is the final destination on Bonita Canyon highway. Massai Point was originally called by the Apache *Say Yahdesut*, meaning "Point of Rocks." The Apache believed that after they died, their souls remained at this hallowed ground. Massai Point reaches an elevation of 6,700 feet. The area consists of a broad open plateau that provides excellent views of the rock formations throughout the monument. The area also includes improvements such as a picnic area, restroom and interpretive exhibit building. Built in 1939 by the National Park Service, the Interpretive Exhibit Building consists of rhyolite mortar quarried at a nearby location, perhaps at the higher northwest slope of Garfield Peak, and erected so as to blend in with the surrounding landscape.

Additional trails in the Chiricahua Mountains outside the monument are found off the Crest Trail, accessible from Pinery Canyon Road. At the first evidence of snow in November in the higher elevations, the western portion of Pinery Canyon Road from East Turkey Creek Road to the Forest Boundary may be closed because of snow accumulation. It is recommended to contact the Douglas Ranger District for details. Forest Road #42 is the same as Pinery Canyon Road.

The Crest Trail begins around Buena Vista Peak at 8,823 feet and provides access to Monte Vista Peak, Sentinel Peak and Rustler Park, traveling in a southward direction for twelve miles at an elevation above 9,000 feet. Along the trail in either an east or west direction, extensions of other trails are visibly apparent, making the Crest Trail an integral part of a system of trails that leads to a number of important points of interest, including Centella Point, Chiricahua Peak and Fly Peak. Accessibility is located on the west side of Rustler Park Campground, open from April through November and closed during the winter because of snow and ice storms. The Crest Trail is considered the longest trail in the Chiricahua Mountain Range. The Crest Trail provides access to the Barfoot Lookout at an elevation of 8,823 feet. The lookout, built in 1935, was listed on the National Historic Lookout Register. Unfortunately, it was destroyed on June 3, 2011, by embers from the Horseshoe 2 Fire that breeched the fire-retardant materials that had been used to protect it.

One can reach the summit by traversing the Crest Trail for five miles. Prior to the Horseshoe 2 Fire in 2011, the Rattlesnake Fire in 1994 burned 27,500 acres, including large parts of the trail, which now appear like some of the more notable World War I battlefields like the Marne and Somme. Water is often accessible at nearby Booger Spring and Anita Spring on the journey to Chiricahua Peak. *Centella*, a Spanish word, is translated in English to mean "lightning spangles." A name aptly applied to Centella Point, where evidence of lightning strikes appears in the scarred ponderosa pines. A former forest service tower in the area was named "Thunderbolt."

One of the taller peaks found in the southern Chiricahua Mountains is Monte Vista Peak. It rises 9,357 feet and is accessible from the North Fork Trail in Rucker Canyon. Located in the Chiricahua Wilderness, the trail covers a distance of 7.8 miles round trip and takes an average of six hours to hike through the pine-oak woodland. Monte Vista Peak hosts a spectacular view of Rucker Canyon and the surrounding valleys of southeastern Arizona down into Mexico.

The Rucker Canyon Trail is a 5.6-mile round trip averaging a hiking time of three hours. Because Rucker Canyon is part of the drainage of Chiricahua Peak, the highest point in the mountains, Rucker Canyon Creek is subject to flash floods during the summer months. Upper Rucker Canyon contains a notable gorge enclosed with walls of rhyolite attaining heights in excess of six hundred feet.

The Silver Peak Trail is a popular hike on the east side of the Chiricahua Mountains. This four-and-a-half-mile trail begins two miles up the road from Portal in Cave Creek Canyon, only a short distance from the Cave Creek Visitor Information Center. It ascends a 3,000-foot climb to a 7,975-foot summit covering rugged and, at times, challenging terrain with numerous switchbacks. The hike covers desert grassland and concludes in a forest of Douglas fir. The views from the summit are rewarding, including those to the east of the San Simon Valley, the Peloncillo Mountains and into New Mexico. The eastern slopes of the Chiricahua Mountains present an amazing sight, including Cave Creek, East Turkey Creek and South Fork of Cave Creek that precipitate out of the mountain range. The remains of the Silver Peak Lookout, destroyed in a fire on October 1992, are also present.

The South Fork Trail, known as #243, consists of seven and a half miles of hiking trails along with a picnic area, a restroom and a parking lot at the trailhead. It is accessible three and a half miles west of Portal and is popular among birders who are seeking out elegant trogons, redfaced warblers and painted redstarts. The trail ascends 3,600 feet in elevation and includes several streambeds that run with water depending on rainfall and snowmelt. As a caveat to hikers, the South Fork area of Cave Creek contains poison ivy. Along the trail, there are a variety of trees that include ash, maples, oaks and sycamore. There are also additional trail junctures, including trail #240, which leads to Horseshoe Saddle and Burro Springs and vista points of South Fork Canyon.

Chapter 14

Vegetation

The diversity of plant life and life zones in the Chiricahua Mountains is exceptional. As the second-highest mountain range in southeastern Arizona, the Chiricahua Mountains include the Upper Sonoran Zone, the Transition Zone and the Canadian Zone. The Upper Sonoran Zone includes grasslands, chapparal and manzanita bush, along with woodland vegetation in the form of juniper, oak and pinyon pine. It generally begins at elevations of 4,500 feet and ends at 6,500 feet. The Transition Zone includes an area that is heavily forested with a mixture of junipers, Gambel oaks, Douglas firs and ponderosa pine trees. Elevation at this level ranges from 6,500 to 8,000 feet. Finally, there is the Canadian Zone, where forests of Douglas fir along with quaking aspen, white fir and blue and Engelmann spruce are abundant. This zone is named for the dense forests of trees similar to those of British Columbia. It is this variety of life zones that enables the Chiricahua Mountains to provide a bridge to similar life zones found in northern Mexico and the American Southwest. These are represented by both the Sonoran and Chihuahuan Deserts and also include similar vegetation found in the Rocky Mountains and also in the Sierra Madre Mountains in Mexico. Apache Pass is often considered a border between two biomes: the Sonoran and the Chihuahuan Deserts. Apache Spring still contains water to this day.

A visit to Chiricahua National Monument gives a greater appreciation for the diversity of trees commonly seen along Bonita Canyon Highway. The mouth of Bonita Canyon is characterized as oak-woodland. The road parallels Bonita Creek between the entrance and the campground. Some of these trees include silverleaf and emory oaks, Chihuahua pine, Arizona cypress, Apache pine and alligator juniper. Some of these trees grow in excess of seventy-five feet in height. Mexican pinyon pine, Manzanita bushes and chaparral are abundant on Sugarloaf Mountain, while a yucca grassland environment is found on its southern slope. Bracken fern are common along areas of the Crest Trail in the higher elevations of the Chiricahua Mountains. Multiple colors of pine-leaf Penstemon ranging from yellow, purple and red are also found.

The Chiricahua Mountains are known to have rare plants that, in certain cases, are only indigenous to that mountain range. Chiricahua fleabane is a wildflower endemic only to the Chiricahua Mountains. It grows best on north-facing granite cliffs and rock ledges surrounded by moss and lichens. Purple Mountain Rocky Iris, delphinium and sunflowers appear in Rustler Park during the summer months. Violets and geraniums are also found in Rustler Park. Some of the less common species of plants found in the Chiricahua Mountains include *Apacheria chiricahuensis*, an endemic species of plant discovered in 1973 that is found exclusively on the south-facing cliffs in the Chiricahua Mountains. Apache pine is only found in southeastern Arizona, southwestern New Mexico and northern Mexico. It is therefore a rather uncommon pine. Apache pine can attain heights of up to seventy-five feet and a base of twenty-five inches in diameter. Its long, drooping needles are dark green, usually three to a bundle. The needles of the Apache pine are not as dark green as those of the ponderosa pine. Apache pine has preferred elevation ranges from between five thousand and eight thousand feet. They have light-brown cones averaging three to four inches in length and have a life span averaging four hundred to five hundred years.

Several additional rare species of plants include the Chiricahua Mountain tansy-aster, which occurs most notably in the Willcox Playa. Another rare plant is Hinckley's polemonium. Although this species grows in Big Bend, Texas, and parts of Mexico, the Chiricahua Mountains are its only documented locality in Arizona. It grows in higher wooded terrain that includes ponderosa pine and Douglas fir. Another plant of limited distribution is *Gentianella wislizeni*, also known as the Chiricahua Mountain dwarf gentian. It also grows in higher elevation area, which includes pine-oak woodland. It flowers in the summer and is most often seen in areas that have received a low-intensity burn from a forest fire. Many of these rare plants are grazed by cattle, making seed distribution challenging.

Trees found in the Chiricahua Mountains produce seeds that are eaten by wildlife. Seeds are also dispersed by wind, leading to the natural propagation of trees, especially in areas that have suffered from forest fire in the past. The ponderosa pine is the most common species of pine in Arizona. It is also a highly sought after source of lumber used in the construction of houses and furniture. It reaches a height of 125 feet with a trunk up to 4 feet in diameter. The dark-green needles appear in bundles of three and five and reach up to seven inches long. Some of these trees can live in excess of four hundred years if they are not prematurely killed by disease or lightning. A feature that protects these trees from wind damage is the twist wood beneath their bark.

Additional trees found in the Chiricahua Mountains include Douglas fir, quaking aspen and juniper. The Douglas fir can reach heights up to 130 feet in the Chiricahua Mountains and is considered the largest tree in Arizona. Its trunk averages 4 feet in diameter. Quaking aspen are another tree found among the ponderosa pines and spruce forests in the Chiricahua Mountains. Aspen seeds need consistently moist soil to germinate and are therefore found in higher elevations with greater precipitation. They are conspicuous in the fall, when their leaves change color to golden yellow or orange before they drop from the tree. They will reappear again in the spring. The leaves serve as a food source for beavers and deer. They also produce a distinct sound or cadence when affected by the wind. Quaking aspen attain heights on average of 60 feet with a 1-foot diameter at their trunk. The Chiricahua Mountains are one of the southernmost regions in North America where Engelmann spruce are found. Engelmann spruce in Arizona attain a height less than 100 feet with dark-green to pale blue-green needles. Their bark appears purplish to reddish brown.

Several different types of juniper trees grow in the Chiricahua Mountains, including the alligator juniper and the one-seed juniper. The alligator juniper can attain a height of fifty feet with a trunk four feet in diameter. It is named after the deep one- to two-inch square fissures evident in the tree's bark, which appears to resemble the hide of an alligator. It is the largest species of juniper in Arizona. This evergreen tree produces berries that sustain wildlife. Its cones are reddish brown and half an inch in diameter. The average life of this tree is five hundred years, although some can live in excess of one thousand years. The leaves are bluish green and scale-like, growing in dense clusters on branches. The one-seed juniper, in comparison, is much smaller, obtaining a maximum height of around twenty-five feet. Its trunk is one and a half feet in diameter. Its leaves are yellowish green and scale-like, and its cones appear red at maturity.

The silverleaf oak is a white-leaf oak that can obtain a height of sixty feet with a trunk two and a half feet in diameter. It often blooms between April and May at elevations of five thousand to seven thousand feet in Arizona mountain slopes and oak woodlands. It produces acorns. It derives its name from its leaf coloration, which ranges from yellow-green to silver-white.

Arizona cypress are the most numerous in Rucker Canyon. They grow at elevations between 3,500 feet and 5,500 feet in canyons and slopes. This evergreen tree produces cones that are reddish brown in color and remain on the tree for several years. The Arizona cypress is noted for its rough bark. It attains a height of 40 feet with a trunk 2 feet in diameter.

Cave Creek possesses the most abundant water supply in the Chiricahua Mountains. It receives water from nearby creeks and streams, including Cima and North Fork Creeks, along with streams from South Fork and Snowshed Canyons. Because of the riparian qualities of Cave Creek, the area supports a diverse collection of trees, including ash, cherry, cottonwoods, big-tooth maples, poplar, sycamore and walnuts. All of these trees make the Cave Creek area a splendid site to visit during the autumn when the colors are changing.

Many of the plants found in the Chiricahua Mountains were used by Native Americans and early American settlers as sources of sustenance and building material. Wood from the native trees was used to fuel fire and was also used to build fences and homes. Wood from trees like the quaking aspen was used in the manufacture of paper pulp. Some of the plants contained medicinal applications. They also provided a shelter for animals and birds seeking to escape the harsh elements during certain times of the year. The sotol plant found in the Chiricahua Mountains was used by the Chiricahua Apache as sustenance. They broke apart the head to acquire the food inside, which has a taste similar to raw cabbage. The heads or hearts were roasted or eaten raw. The long spiny blades are similar to pineapple. A strong alcoholic beverage can be acquired from the juices of sotol. Beargrass (*Nolina erumpens*) was also known as basketgrass because both the Indians and Mexicans fashioned basketry using the fiber from the leaves. Ropes, sandals and matting were also fashioned out of the same material.

Lichens appear frequently on the rock pinnacles in the Chiricahua Mountains. They appear in colors ranging from green to white, orange and red and add richness and contrast to the rocks when viewed from a distance. They also cause weathering in the rock face through chemical and physical processes. Lichens produce acids that leach into the rocks, producing an etching effect as temperature fluctuation and water cause the host rock to chip and disintegrate, weakening the overall structure. This leads to a gradual erosion/decomposition of the rock over time. Lichens are composed of colonies of algae and fungi that live together on the surface of

Cochise Head is covered by a dense blanket of ponderosa pines in this spectacular view. Named after the Apache Indian chief Cochise, this prominent rock formation attains a height of 8,109 feet. *Courtesy of William Ascarza.*

the rock in a symbiotic relationship. Over time, they produce rock varnish, a combination of iron and manganese on the rock surface. Rock varnish produces a mineral patina on the surface of a rock that appears in brown and black blotches. The minerals are composed of clays including illite, kaolinite and montmorillonite. These minerals are mixed with a combination of iron and manganese oxides that slowly accumulate after a rainfall. Its thickness varies, averaging less than a hundredth of an inch on the host rock.

Chapter 15

Ranching

Cattle were first introduced into southern Arizona by the Spanish explorer Francisco Vasquez de Coronado in 1540. The Coronado Expedition, consisting of three hundred men, brought 150 cattle into the land that today is known as Arizona. The Spanish Jesuit explorer Father Francisco Kino later established several missions at Guevavi, Tumacocori and San Xavier, introducing several thousand head of cattle to the region and becoming Arizona's first cattle baron during the early 1700s. It was Father Kino who instructed the local Indians on how to ranch. The Spanish government provided large land grants to enhance the Spanish cattle industry, which suffered setbacks because of the raiding Apache. It was not until the arrival of the United States after the Gadsden Purchase of 1853 that cattle ranching became more prevalent with the introduction of Texas longhorns, Brahmas and Herefords. Hereford cattle were popular because of their adaptability to an arid climate. Ranching in southeastern Arizona was initially an extension of ranching in West Texas. Texas ranchers, weary of threats to the open range including restrictive land laws, homesteaders and drought, sought to improve their lot by extending their ranches farther west. Beginning in the 1840s, ranchers from Texas would traverse the land that today is Arizona on their way to the cattle market in California, where they could maximize profits. The advance of the railroad into Arizona by 1880 and the access to the cattle market to the south in the Mexican states of Chihuahua and Sonora made cattle ranching enticing in southeastern Arizona. The demand for beef from military outposts and reservations such as Fort Bowie and San

Carlos also greatly benefitted the ranching enterprise. Abundant grassland, some of which was knee-deep, in the surrounding Sulphur Spring Valley, San Simon Valley and San Bernardino Valley captured the interests of eastern and midwestern ranchers. While San Simon Valley, located east of the mountains, has experienced an influx of population growth over the past several decades, Sulfur Springs Valley to the west has remained rural and dominated by farmland. While cattlemen from Texas brought seasoned experience to the rangeland in southeastern Arizona, they also brought their share of ranching problems, including overstocking and disease, which, along with homesteading, had reduced the large ranches in southeastern Arizona by the early twentieth century.

The increase in livestock grazing in the Sulphur Spring Valley in the 1870s brought about an increase in cattle rustling. Many of the cattle rustlers, such as Curly Bill Brocius and Johnny Ringo, sought to establish roving bases of operations across the Chiricahua Mountains. One such area was the town of Galeyville. Another such area was Rustler Park, located four miles from Onion Saddle on Forest Service Road 42 D. Rustler Park was named after the cattle thieves who used the area surrounded by ponderosa pine, including Barfoot Park, as a hideout in the 1880s. The rustlers maintained a stock of stolen cattle at this locality prior to selling them to local ranchers in the valley.

A typical forest service cabin as seen in Rustler Park 1937. *Courtesy of United States Department of Agriculture.*

Sulphur Springs Valley was known as Sulphur Spring Valley until the early twentieth century—named for the two springs located in the middle of the valley a mile west of "Three Sisters" or "Three Nuns," large hills near what is known today as Kansas Settlement. The Sulphur Spring Valley included four prominent ranches in the late 1880s, including the Chiricahua Cattle Company in the north and the Erie Cattle Company in the south, along with the Kansas Cattle Company and the Tombstone Land and Cattle Company. By the mid-1880s, with the Apache removed and dispersed in Florida and New Mexico, ranchers could maintain large herds of cattle on the grassland at little cost. Many of the cattle rustlers prevalent in the 1870s and early 1880s were captured or killed by local law enforcement. Removal of these impediments allowed for increased ranching in the region. The arrival of the railroad to southeastern Arizona in the early 1880s provided ranchers with a means to transport their cattle to market. The long cattle drives became less of a factor, and low railroad freight fees became a more popular means of negotiation. The town of Willcox became renowned in the cattle shipping industry. By 1898, there were over seventeen thousand brands of cattle in Arizona. The practice of branding cattle dates back several thousand years to the Egyptian, Greek and Roman eras. The first branding of cattle in the New World was conducted by Hernando Cortes after the demise of the Aztec Empire.

As more ranches became established, the ranchers contributed more funds and influence toward the necessity of law enforcement. John H. Slaughter, a rancher himself and a stalwart supporter of the need to eradicate rustlers, became sheriff of Cochise County on the pledge of removing the rustling element. The Arizona Rangers, created in 1901 and patterned after the Texas Rangers, had a similar purpose to track, capture or kill rustlers free of the hindrance of county lines. The establishment of the Arizona Cattle Growers Association in 1904 aided the small force of twenty-six Arizona Rangers in local law enforcement.

Several renowned Cochise County ranches include the Erie Cattle Company, established in the summer of 1883, and the Chiricahua Cattle Company, established in the spring of 1885. Combined, they controlled 1,000,000 acres in the Sulphur Springs Valley. The former occupied the southern end of the valley, while the northern end was occupied by the latter. The Chiricahua Cattle Company, known as the 3C's, acquired 1,658,880 acres of public land, making it one of the largest ranching operations in Arizona. The Chiricahua Cattle Company, a powerful outfit, was awarded the contract by the U.S. military to supply 900,000 pounds of beef annually to the San Carlos and

White Mountains Apache Reservations in May 1892; it also supplied beef to the U.S. military and the United States as a whole. John Vickers and his brother Sumner Vickers, along with Theodore White, were the creators of the Chiricahua Cattle Company. Thomas F. White, a government surveyor, and his brothers Jarett and Theodore were strong proponents of the cattle industry in southeastern Arizona, and they established their headquarters at the El Dorado Ranch on the western slope of the Chiricahua Mountains, where the waters from Turkey Creek enter the Sulphur Spring Valley.

During the last half of the nineteenth century, the San Simon Valley was described as some of the richest cattle grazing land in the West. The San Simon Cattle and Canal Company was created by James Parramore in 1883, in partnership of Hugh Lewis and Claiborne W. Merchant. The San Simon Cattle and Canal Company continued to buy up water rights in the San Simon Valley and into western New Mexico. It did so in a noncontiguous fashion, which left the land to be divided up into parcels, making it easier for it to become subdivided by the mid-twentieth century. The San Simon Cattle and Canal Company was commonly referred to as the H's or 7H because of its habit of branding the letter *H* on the cattle.

James Harrison Parramore was born on August 13, 1840, in Early County, Georgia, though he grew up in Mississippi and Texas. He served in the Eighth Texas Cavalry, attaining the rank of captain during the War Between the States. He saw action at Shiloh and Chickamauga. After the war, he journeyed to Texas, expanding his cattle empire of Texas longhorns into New Mexico and eventually southeastern Arizona. Parramore supported laws that protected the cattle industry and served on many cattle committees. He was influential in the establishment of Rodeo, New Mexico, which served as a cattle shipping station along the El Paso and Southwestern Railroad. By 1888, the San Simon Cattle and Canal Company controlled several thousand acres of land east of the Chiricahua Mountains, running over fifteen thousand head of cattle while shipping half that number back east using the railroad to help satisfy the country's growing need for beef. The spring of 1891 was an excellent one for Parramore and his San Simon Cattle and Canal Company, having branded fifteen thousand calves. The San Simon Cattle and Canal Company lasted nearly forty years. It ranged the valley from the Chiricahua Mountains to the Peloncillo Mountains. It evicted squatters from the land by paying them in silver or by using force. Parramore, who decided to leave Arizona because of the increase in homesteaders, died in 1917. His son Dock Dillworth Parramore ran the ranch for several years before selling.

A portrait of James Parramore, cattle and water baron of the San Simon Valley on the eastern flank of the Chiricahua Mountains. *Courtesy of Hardin-Simmons Photograph Collection.*

Another prominent rancher mentioned earlier who made his presence felt in Cochise County was John Slaughter, a Confederate veteran who hailed from Texas. John Slaughter served as an Indian fighter, Texas Ranger and sheriff of Tombstone. His keen tracking skills brought him to the Chiricahua Mountains when searching for renegade Apache and outlaws. Slaughter arrived in Arizona with a herd of longhorns. Shortly thereafter, he purchased part of the San Bernardino Land Grant in 1884, forming the San Bernardino Ranch. The land grant dated back to 1822, when the Mexican government deeded 73,240 acres to Ignacio Perez, who remained at ranch for only a decade, forced to leave the area due to Apache deprivations. Part of the original land grant would later be acquired by the United States following the Gadsden Purchase of 1853. Over the next several decades, the Apache threat was greatly impeded by the U.S. military and the influx of settlement. Slaughter would continue to acquire land for his massive cattle enterprise. He would eventually acquire over 100,000 acres. Several U.S. cavalry encampments were established at the site on Slaughter's land to protect settlements along the border during World I in response to the instability in Mexico, including the raids of Pancho Villa. All that remains of their existence today are scattered rock fortifications.

John Slaughter's San Bernardino Ranch is located seventeen miles east of Douglas. The San Bernardino Ranch land, covering southeastern Arizona and northern Mexico, served as prime real estate for cattle ranching and farming until it was acquired by the Nature Conservancy in 1979. The San Bernardino Ranch is now a public attraction with holdings divided between the Nature Conservancy and the San Bernardino National Wildlife Refuge. Operated by the Floyd Johnson Foundation, the museum includes

John Slaughter, ex–Texas Ranger and renowned sheriff of Cochise County, made many forays into the Chiricahua Mountains in search of Apache and outlaws. He owned the San Bernardino ranch, seventeen miles east of Douglas, and was instrumental in the town's formation. He was a cattle baron running thousands of head of cattle on his massive ranch that extended down into Mexico. Slaughter branded his cattle with a *Z*, which was one of the earliest brands registered in Cochise County. *Courtesy of* Who's Who in Arizona.

the original ranch building built by John Slaughter, as well as manmade ponds and nearby army camp ruins dating back to the days of Pancho Villa.

The decline in ranching in southeastern Arizona during the 1890s was brought about by several factors: overgrazing, disease, the drought of 1891–92, hard freezes, fences, railroad cost and the influx of homesteaders in the valley who chose to dry farm, as well as other ventures such as mining and dams. Challenges to the cattle industry included the volatility of the cattle market and fluctuating weather conditions coupled with the decrease of availability of water to support the massive herds. Artesian wells were in high demand, especially when the territorial Arizona legislature in 1875 offered a sum of $3,000 for anyone who could come forth and produce evidence of their existence in Arizona. Diseases emanating from the Texas rangeland such as pleuropneumonia and "tick fever" spread among Texas longhorns, necessitating the need to quarantine in Arizona, a practice sanctioned by northern and northwestern states. Because of the severity of the drought in 1891 and 1892, ranchers lost 50 to 75 percent of their cattle by the summer of 1893. Bunch, grama and sacaton are some of the grasses that supplied the cattle industry in Sulphur Spring Valley during the 1880s. Over 1 million acres of grassland were destroyed by fifty thousand head of cattle in the Sulphur Spring Valley by the early 1890s, causing some Arizona ranchers to move their operation to the grasslands of Oklahoma, Kansas and back

Above and below: A modern-day view of the Slaughter Ranch, located fifteen miles east of Douglas on the Geronimo Trail. In its heyday in 1884, it encompassed over 100,000 acres. Today, 300 acres have been preserved. The pond was built by John Slaughter using the available water from natural springs. The San Bernardino National Wildlife Refuge stocks the pond with Yaqui catfish, chub and topminnow. *Courtesy of William Ascarza.*

to Texas. Overgrazing by cattle reduced the available grassland, which, once impacted, was slow to recover. Mesquite trees, chaparral and other invasive species proved difficult to remove once established.

By 1902, with the establishment of the Chiricahua Forest Reserve, water and land management became more regulated between the federal government and the ranchers. Deflation and the decline of beef exports plagued the remaining ranches after World War I. Today, there are efforts to rejuvenate the grasslands that once surrounded the Chiricahua Mountains. With his neighboring ranchers, Warner Glenn formed the Malpai Borderlands Group in 1994, a nonprofit organization whose purpose through collaboration is to better manage 1 million acres of land in southeastern Arizona and bordering southwestern New Mexico. The group has partnered with several government agencies, including the U.S. Department of Agriculture, U.S. Department of Interior and the U.S. Department of Homeland Security. The area of coverage of the group includes over 800,000 acres of land extending from the base of the Chiricahua Mountains to the Playas Valley in Southwest New Mexico.

Guest ranches became increasingly popular in and around the Chiricahua Mountains beginning with the Faraway Ranch run by the Erickson family, mentioned in the homesteading chapter earlier. Civilian Conservation Corps Camp NM-2-A operated on this acreage, which included the Silver Spur Meadow. A mixture of buildings was erected, including wooden barracks, work shops, offices and residences. The mess hall served as the main lodge of what later became the Silver Spur Guest Ranch. Purchased by William Sprague in 1945, the ranch remained in operation for two years and then was purchased in 1949 by Ray Kent, who continued the tradition of operating the building as the Silver Spur Guest Ranch until 1967, when the Kent family sold their holding to the National Park Service. In 1971, the National Park Service dismantled the buildings on the site, leaving two large stone fireplaces that remain in existence today.

The area known as Sunglow, named by Jeff P. Thomason Sr. for the warm golden glow of the sun in the area in the early morning, is located near the Chiricahua Mountains and is well known for a guest ranch by that same name. The Sunglow Ranch encompasses 475 acres of land with ten guest casitas. Bordering Coronado National Forest, it is a popular site for overnight guests who visit to experience horseback riding, hiking, night sky viewing and bird-watching. Johnny Ringgold, also known as Johnny Ringo, the outlaw of Tombstone notoriety, is buried near the locality of Sunglow. Some sources say he committed suicide several hundred feet from where

The post office and next-door library buildings provide small-town charm to Portal, Arizona. *Courtesy of William Ascarza.*

he was shot, while others believe him to have been slain due to the fact that Ringo's revolver contained all its shells at the inquest of the coroner's jury. His body was found propped up against a tree with a bullet in his head.

Although not a ranch per se, the Portal Peak Lodge is one of the top recommended sites in the Chiricahua Mountains. Located at the mouth of Cave Creek Canyon in the town of Portal and behind the Portal Store & Café, the lodge includes fully furnished guest rooms to accommodate many of the visitors who actively bird and hike on the east side of the Chiricahua Mountains.

Conclusion

Despite the impact of the Horseshoe 2 Fire and their remote status in southeastern Arizona, the Chiricahua Mountains will continue to attract visitors. Their unique rock formations, dense patches of forest, ease of accessibility and diverse natural and ecological history make this range an essential visit in southeastern Arizona. The balanced rocks, spectacular views, creeks, campsites, open range and proximity to both Mexico and New Mexico offer an alluring and enticing destination getaway.

As one of the more remote locations in southeastern Arizona, the Chiricahua Mountains have retained a reputation of a rugged yet vastly untouched landscape. They have been the scene of television shows and *Fire on the Chiricahua Mountains*, a film that premiered in 1956 starring John Bromfield. The film depicted three convicts escaping while fighting a forest fire. More recently, Bear Grylls, the famous survivalist from the United Kingdom, visited the Chiricahua Mountains and the surrounding valley. The episode from his popular survival reality show *Man vs. Wild* was aptly named "Arizona Sky Islands." In this episode, Bear Grylls navigates the unique rock formations of the Chiricahua Mountains and builds a dune buggy from the remains of an aircraft in the wilderness of the desert landscape.

Unfortunately, modern-day challenges have caught up with the Chiricahua Mountains. The area is the site of human trafficking and drug trade. Although not considered as dangerous as the border perimeter between Arizona and Mexico, there is enough of a criminal element to condone a U.S. Border Patrol presence. The effects of light pollution are felt to a certain degree in the Chiricahua Mountains. Despite the popularity of using sodium vapor lights in southeastern Arizona towns and cities, the effects are far-reaching. Tucson emits enough light that it can be seen in the northwestern horizon from the vantage point of the Chiricahua Mountains. However, the night sky viewing in the Chiricahua Mountains remains some of the best in southeastern Arizona.

There are many excellent localities in the Chiricahua Mountains from which to stargaze. In the boundaries of the national monument, the Echo Canyon parking lot is one of the best because of its ability to provide the viewer a 320-degree view of the sky with the main obstacle being Sugarloaf Mountain. However, this obstacle can also benefit the viewer because it blocks out the sky glow of Tucson in the distance. The summer Milky Way is absolutely astounding when viewed with the naked eye or perhaps a pair of binoculars. Distant galaxies such as Andromeda and our own galaxy, the Milky Way, are crisp and attractive when the sky is steady. Despite the potential of wind that can, on certain days, appear overbearing, there are quite a few evenings out of the year that are calm and inviting to stargazers in the Chiricahua Mountains.

The smelter town of Douglas, Arizona, was established in 1901 by Phelps Dodge. It was named after mining engineer James Douglas, president of Phelps Dodge Corporation, who was successful in promoting mining operations in Bisbee. Ore from Bisbee and Nacozari in Sonora was shipped to Douglas via the El Paso and Southwestern Railroad. Seen here in the 1920s, the Grand Theater is on the left and the several-story Gadsden Hotel is on the distant right. *Courtesy of Freeport-McMoRan.*

Opposite, bottom: The running waters of Cave Creek provide a restful respite from the daily turmoil of the modern world. *Courtesy of William Ascarza.*

The original Hotel Gadsden, built in 1907, was billed as the "best hotel in the West." A five-story, 160-room structure, the Gadsden Hotel was where cattle kings and mining barons held meetings while securing multimillion-dollar deals. During the Mexican Revolution, the roof of the Gadsden offered spectators a view of the battle between Pancho Villa's forces against those of the Federales at Agua Prieta, with the caveat of an occasional stray bullet. The hotel burned in a fire in 1927 and was subsequently rebuilt in even grander fashion in 1929. It remains operational to this day. *Courtesy of* Who's Who in Arizona.

A table at the Interpretive Exhibit Building at Massai Point denotes dark skies in Arizona as some of the best in the United States, with the exception of those affected by light pollution from nearby major cities in Arizona, such as Phoenix, Tucson and Sierra Vista. The Chiricahua Mountains can certainly boast some of the best night sky viewing in the state. They are one among a handful of national parks and monuments that possess a rich dark sky—the darkest of which in the lower forty-eight states is Big Bend National Park in Texas, whose horizon in totally untouched by the lights of man. The nearest major light polluting city affecting the Chiricahua Mountains is Sierra Vista, located ninety miles by vehicle to the west. *Courtesy of William Ascarza.*

Additional recommended places from which to view the night sky include the Pinery Canyon Campground. When open, its views are unimpeded due in large part to the effects of the Horseshoe 2 Fire on the trees in the vicinity. The Cave Creek area around Portal, though surrounded by mountainous terrain, provides dark skies void of the distant light glow of Tucson and Sierra Vista to the west. Rucker Canyon to the southeast also appears to boast dark skies that may only contend with the light pollution of Douglas to the southeast.

The Chiricahua Mountains are a time machine to the past in the present. They are a range well worth visiting, one that is memorable. The views alone are worth a day trip. Lack of development, open land and big sky country are plentiful. The crackle of static from the radio waves in the ether in the Chiricahua Mountains will tell visitors they are in distant country, far away from civilization. Drive out and explore. An adventure awaits.

Bibliography

Aircraft Wrecks in Arizona and the Southwest. "AT-17B #42-38739 History of Flight." www.aircraftarchaeology.com.

———. "OS2U Kingfisher Crash." www.aircraftarchaeology.com/OS2UKingfisherCrash.htm.

Bailey, Lynn Robison. *We'll All Wear Silk Hats: The Erie and Chiricahua Cattle Companies and the Rise of Corporate Ranching in the Sulphur Spring Valley of Arizona, 1883–1909*. Tucson, AZ: Westernlore Press, 1994.

Barnes, Will C. *Arizona Place Names*. Tucson: University of Arizona Press, 1960.

Bigsby, P.R. "Mineral Investigation of the North End Roadless area, Cochise County, Arizona." U.S. Bureau of Mines Mineral Land Assessment MLA 1-83. Denver, CO: Bureau of Mines, Department of the Interior, 1983.

Brandes, Ray. "A Guide to the History of the U.S. Army Installations in Arizona, 1849–1886." *Journal of the Southwest* 1, no. 1 (Spring 1959): 42–65.

Brown, S.D. "Mineral Appraisal of the Coronado National Forest: Part 2, Chiricahua-Pedregosa Mountains Unit, Cochise County, Arizona." Intermountain Field Operations Center, Denver, Colorado, 1993.

CBS 5 AZ KPHO. "Small Plane Crashes in SE Arizona; 2 Die 8-26-2010." www.kpho.com/story/14790592/small-plane-crashes-in-se-arizona-2-die-8-26-2010.

Chapel, William L. "Camp Rucker: Outpost in Apacheria." *Journal of Arizona History* 14, no. 2 (Summer 1973): 95–112.

Chiricahua Mountains, Arizona: A Trail and Recreation Map. 5th edition. Tucson, AZ: Rainbow Expeditions, 1991.

Chiricahua National Monument, Arizona. National Park Service U.S. Department of the Interior brochure.

Chronic, Halka. *Roadside Geology of Arizona*. Missoula, MT: Mountain Press Publishing Company, 1983.

"The Civilian Conservation Corps Coronado National Forest 1933–1942." Prepared by Forest Servest United States Department of Agriculture U.S. Government Printing Office 1997-573-252/24078.

Cochise Quarterly 12, no. 1. "Ranch Life, The Border Country 1880–1940: The Way It Really Was." (Spring 1982).

Conners, Jo, comp. *Who's Who in Arizona*. Volume I. Tucson: Press of the Arizona Daily Star, 1913.

Cramer, Harry G., III. "Tom Jeffords: Indian Agent." *Journal of Arizona History* 17, no. 3 (1976).

Dimmitt, M.A., R.C. Brusca, K. Krebbs, C.L. McIntyre, J. Viers, C. Filippone and A. Berry. *Natural Resource Condition Assessment: Chiricahua National Monument, Coronado National Memorial, and Fort Bowie National Historic Site.* Tucson: Arizona-Sonora Desert Museum and Sonoran Institute, 2011.

Dorr, L.L. "The Fight at Chiricahua Pass in 1869." *Journal of the Southwest* 13, no. 4 (Winter 1971).

Drewes, Harald, and Frank E. Williams. "Mineral Resources of the Chiricahua Wilderness Area, Cochise County, Arizona." *Geological Survey Bulletin* 1385-A. Washington, D.C.: U.S. Government Printing Office, 1973.

Elsing, Morris J., and Robert E.S. Heineman. "Arizona Metal Production." *Arizona Bureau of Mines, Economic Series,* no. 19, bulletin no. 140 (1936).

Epple, Anne Orth. *A Field Guide to the Plants of Arizona*. Helena, MT: Falcon Press Publishing Co., Inc., 1995.

Faulk, Odie B. *Arizona A Short History*. Norman: University of Oklahoma Press, 1970.

Gee, Henry. *Rise of the Dragon: Readings from Nature on the Chinese Fossil Record.* Chicago: University of Chicago Press, 2002.

Glenn, Warner. *Eyes on Fire: Encounters with a Borderland Jaguar*. El Paso, TX: Printing Corner Press, 1996.

Goodwin, Grenville, and Neil Goodwin. *The Apache Diaries: A Father-Son Journey*. Lincoln: University of Nebraska Press, 2000.

"Gould's Turkeys Making a Comeback in Arizona." U.S. Federal News Service, January 13, 2006.

Graham, J. "Chiricahua National Monument Geologic Resources Inventory Report." Natural Resource Report NPS/NRPC/GRD/NRR-2009/081. Denver, CO: National Park Service, 2009.

Hadley, Diana. "Landholding Systems and Resource Management in the Sky Island Borderlands." USDA Forest Service Proceedings RMRS-P-36, 2005.

Hayes, Alden. *A Portal to Paradise.* Tucson: University of Arizona Press, 1999.

Hayes, Alden C., and Karen Hayes. "Sierra Madre Revisted." *Journal of Arizona History* 32, no. 2 (Summer 1992): 125–52.

Heald, Weldon F. *Sky Island*. Princeton, NJ: D. Van Nostrand Company, 1967.

Herman, George R. "A Bad Day at Douglas Army Airfield." *Journal of Arizona History* 36, no. 4 (Winter 1995): 367–92.

Historic American Buildings Survey, Faraway Ranch, Stafford Riggs Cabin, HABS No. AZ-139-B.

Hoppe, Eleanor Sellers. "Parramore, James Harrison." Handbook of Texas Online http://www.tshaonline.org/handbook/online/articles/fpa37, accessed February 27, 2013. Published by the Texas State Historical Association.

Huachuca Illustrated: A Magazine of the Fort Huachuca Museum, Fort Huachuca and the Geronimo Campaign 1886 7 (1999). http://huachuca-www.army.mil/Files/History_Illustrated_Geronimo.pdf.

Jaguar Conservation Team Borderlands Conservation Strategy for the Northern Jaguar Draft. January 2006.

Keith, Stanton B. "Index of Mining Properties in Cochise County, Arizona." *Arizona Bureau of Mines Bulletin* 187 (1973).

Lamberton, Ken. *Chiricahua Mountains Bridging the Borders of Wilderness*. Tucson: University of Arizona Press, 2003.

Lucchitta, Ivo. *Hiking Arizona's Geology*. Seattle, WA: Mountaineers Books, 2001.

Lynch, D.J. "The San Bernardino Volcanic Field of Southeastern Arizona." In *Land of Cochise*, edited by Callender, J.F., J. Wilt, R.E. Clemons and H.L. James. New Mexico Geological Society Guidebook, 29th Field Conference.

Massey, Peter, Jeanne Wilson and Angela Titus. *Arizona Trails, South Region*. Castle Rock, CO: Adler Publishing, 2007.

McGarvin, T.G. "The 1887 Sonoran Earthquake: It Wasn't Our Fault." *Fieldnotes: Arizona Bureau of Geology and Mineral Technology* 17, no. 2 (1987).

Mills, Charles A. *Legends of Lost Treaure.* N.p.: Apple Cheeks Press, 1987.

Milwaukee Sentinel. "Marine Is Killed in Plane Crash." October 13, 1941.

Mine & Quarry 1–5. "Marble Quarrying in Arizona." Published by Sullivan Machinery Company, 1913.

Morris, T. "Work with Jaguars Nets Federal Honor for Douglas Man."*Sierra Vista Herald*, June 13, 2008.

Mulligan, Raymond A. "Sixteen Days in Apache Pass." *The Kiva* 24, no. 2 (December 1958): 1–13.

Murbarger, Nell. *Ghosts of the Adobe Walls*. Los Angeles: Westernlore Press, 1964.

Mustoe, G.E. "The Origin of Honeycomb Weathering." *Geological Society of America Bulletin* 93 (February 1982).

New York Times. "After Plane Crash, Injured Brothers Hike for 4 Days to Safety." November 11, 1990.

NPS Form 10-900. United States Department of the Interior, National Park Service, National Register of Historic Places Registration Form. October 1990.

Paige, Sidney. "Marble Prospects in the Chiricahua Mountains, Arizona." *Bulletin: United States Geological Survey*, issue 380 (1909).

Pallister, J.S., E.A. du Bray and D.B. Hall. "Guide to the Volcanic Geology of Chiricahua National Monument and Vicinity, Cochise County, Arizona." U.S. Dept of Interior, U.S. Geological Survey. Miscellaneous Investigations Series Map I-2541, 1997.

Pearthree, P.A. "Late Quaternary Faulting and Seismic Hazard in Southeastern Arizona and Adjacent Portions of New Mexico and Sonora, Mexico." Arizona Geological Survey, Open-File Report 86-8, 1986.

Peterson, Roger Tory. *A Field Guide to Western Birds*. 3rd edition. Boston: Houghton Mifflin Company, 1990.

Reed, W., M. Schaffner and C. Kahler. "Horseshoe 2 Fire July 15, 2011. Post-Burn Increased Flash Flood Risk Analysis." http://www.cbrfc.noaa.gov/report/horse.pdf.

Romero-Arechederra, Leanndra. "Southwest Fire Science Consortium Field Trip to the Chiricahua National Monument: Discussion of the Impacts of the 2011 Horseshoe 2 Fire." *Arizona Geology Magazine*, December 19, 2012.

Rosen, P.C., C.R. Schwalbe, D.A. Parizek, P.A. Holm and C.H. Lowe. "Introduced Aquatic Vertebrates in the Chiricahua Region: Effects on Declining Native Ranid Frogs." In *Biodiversity and Management of the Madrean Archipelago: The Sky Islands of Southwestern United States and Northwestern Mexico*, L.F. DeBano, et al. (tech. coords.). Fort Collins, CO: USDA, USFS, Rocky Mountain Forest & Range Experimental Sta., General Tech. Report RM-GTR-264, 1995.

Sabins, F.F., Jr. "Stratigraphic Relations in Chiricahua and Dos Cabezas Mountains, Arizona." *AAPG Bulletin* 41, issue 3 (March 1957).

Schreiber, Joseph F., Jr. "Geology of the Willcox Playa, Cochise County, Arizona." New Mexico Geological Society Guidebook, 29th Field Conference, Land of Cochise, 1978. http://nmgs.nmt.edu/publications/guidebooks/downloads/29/29_p0277_p0282.pdf.

Seklecki, M.T., H.D. Grissino-Mayor and H.D. Swetnam. "Fire History and the Possible Role of Apache-Set Fires in the Chiricahua Mountains of Southeastern Arizona." In *Effects of Fire on Madrean Province Ecosystems: A Symposium Proceedings*, L.F. DeBano, et. al. USDA Forest Service General Technical Report RM (1996) 289:238–46.

Sherman, J.E., and B.H. Sherman. *Ghost Towns of Arizona*. Norman: University of Oklahoma Press, 1969.

Snyder, N.F.R, S.E. Koenig, J. Koschmann, H.A. Snyder and T.B. Johnson. "A Journal of Avian Biology: Thick-Billed Parrot Releases in Arizona." *The Condor* 96, no. 4 (November 1994).

Stevens, William K. "Ranchers Ride to the Defense of Mountaintop 'Sky Islands.'" *New York Times*, September 24, 1996.

Sumner, J.R. "The Sonoran Earthquake of 1887." *Bulletin of the Seismological Society of America* 67, no. 4 (1977): 1219–1223.

Suter, Max. "Contemporary Studies of the 3 May 1887 Mw 7.5 Sonora, Mexico (Basin and Range Province) Earthquake." *Seismological Research Letters* 77, no. 2 (March/April 2006).

Sweeney, Edwin R. *From Cochise to Geronimo: The Chiricahua Apaches, 1874–1886.* Norman: University of Oklahoma Press, 2010.

Thrapp, Dan L. *The Conquest of Apacheria.* Norman: University of Oklahoma Press, 1967.

Trachtman, Paul. *The Old West: The Gunfighters.* Alexandria, VA: Time Life Books, 1974.

Trimble, Marshall. *Arizona: A Cavalcade of History*: Tucson, AZ: Treasure Chest Publications, 1989.

———. *Roadside History of Arizona.* Missoula, MT: Mountain Press Publishing Company, 1986.

Tyler, B.A. "Cochise: Apache War Leader 1858–1861." *Journal of Arizona History* 6, no. 1 (Spring 1965).

U.S. Department of the Interior, National Park Service. "The CCC: We Can Take It!" Saguaro National Park. http://www.nps.gov/sagu/planyourvisit/upload/CCCsiteBulletin.pdf.

Utley, Robert Marshall. *Frontier Regulars: The United States Army and the Indian, 1866–1891.* New York: Macmillan, 1973.

Wagoner, Jay J. *Arizona Territory 1863–1912: A Political History.* Tucson: University of Arizona Press, 1970.

Warren, Scott S. *100 Classic Hikes in Arizona.* Seattle, WA: Mountaineers Books, 1994.

Wegman-French, Lysa. Chiricahua National Monument Faraway Ranch Special History Study. Intermountain Cultural Resource Management Professional Paper No. 72, Cultural Resources Division, Intermountain Region, National Park Service, U.S. Department of the Interior, Santa Fe, 2006. http://www.nps.gov/history/history/online_books/chir/special_history.pdf.

White, Brooks. *Galeyville Arizona Territory 1880: Its History and Historic Archaeology.* Raleigh, NC: Pentland Press, Inc., 2000.

Wilson, B.W. "Soldier vs. Apaches: One Last Time at Guadalupe Canyon." *Wild West Magazine,* 2001.

Wilson, Eldred D. "Geology and Ore Deposits of the Courtland-Gleeson Region." *Arizona Bureau of Mines Bulletin* 123 (1927). Tucson, University of Arizona.

Wilson, James A. "West Texas Influence on the Early Cattle Industry of Arizona." *Southwestern Historical Quarterly* 71, no. 1 (July 1967).

About the Author

William Ascarza is an author, entrepreneur, historian, researcher and travel guide. He writes the popular *Arizona Star* column "Mine Tales" about the history of mining in Arizona. He is author of five books, including *Zenith on the Horizon: An Encyclopedic Look at the Tucson Mountains from A to Z*, *Tucson Mountains*, *Sentinel to the North: Exploring the Tortolita Mountains*, *Arizona-Sonora Desert Museum* and *Southeastern Arizona Mining Towns*. As an active member of the Tucson Gem & Mineral Society, he has visited mines across the state and has undertaken extensive research on Arizona's mining history. He is an archivist at the University of Arizona College of Law and leads guided tours across Arizona for Pima Community College, Southwest Trekking and Trail Dust Adventures.